GETTING RESULTS

FIFTY YEARS

OF

OPPORTUNITIES AND DECISIONS

Robert I. Hiller

POPLAR STREET PRESS

Cover by Marianne Hiller

Library of Congress Control Number: 2011929706

First Printing

I.S.B.N. 978-0-615-47753-4 (Hardcover)

1. Hiller, Robert I., 1921- 2. Memoir. 3.History

Published by:
Poplar Street Press, P.O. Box 560605, Charlotte, NC 28256.
E-mail: poplarstpress@bellsouth.net

Dedicated to

my beloved wife of sixty-five years,

MARIANNE

and my children,

<>KAREN KREISBERG <> BARBARA SCHUMAN

<> JOSHUA D. HILLER

and my grandchildren,

<>MICHAEL AND KATHRYN KREISBERG

<> ZEV SCHUMAN OLIVIER

<> SARA SCHUMAN

and

<> ERIC, MARC, AND ALEC HILLER

and My sister in-law,

<>HELEN WEPMAN

TABLE OF CONTENTS

FOREWORD

The period from the end of World War II into the Twenty-first Century was one of extraordinary innovation, growth, and accomplishment in American philanthropy. There are a number of excellent books that chronicle various facets of philanthropy and its development, but Robert Hiller's "professional memoir" truly stands out. It is a fascinating inter-twinning of vision and professional leadership in Jewish philanthropy, coupled with broad personal engagement in innovating, teaching, and guiding philanthropists across the full spectrum of community well being, gender equity, and international social justice.

Many innovations that we take for granted in both tax law and proper management of investing and spending philanthropic dollars originated with Bob Hiller. (Think specifically of United Way, support foundations, and building and using endowment funds for the public good.)

In a very long and successful career, he touched generations of donors and beneficiaries.

I was fortunate to be President of Johns Hopkins University in the 1990's. Bob was fully engaged despite his perennial intent to retire. He seemed a natural ally to assure the future strength of the University by rebuilding the unrestricted endowment of the College of Arts and Sciences. His solution and its implementation (which he describes in the book) were typically ingenious.

When we reach our tenth decade as he has, we may each ask, "What will my legacy be?" We will be fortunate if it is in the neighborhood of Robert Hiller's. And we are fortunate to have his memoir as an inspiration.

William Chase Richardson,
President, Johns Hopkins University, 1990 – 1995; President, W. K. Kellogg Foundation, 1995 – 2005 (2nd largest foundation giving away $250 million per year) Photo courtesy of Ferdinand Hamburger Archives of The Johns Hopkins University.

PROLOGUE

FEW HAVE THIS OPPORTUNITY

As I am but a few months from my Ninetieth Birthday, I cannot believe how fortunate I have been in being part of the history of nearly a century. I've debated with myself as to whether I should wait ten more years, and then write my memoirs. I concluded that it would be wise to settle for ninety percent, because who can predict the next ten percent?

I had never thought of my past as anything but living. I now see it is truly much more than that, because I have had opportunities and made decisions that affected major institutions, total communities, thousands, or perhaps hundreds of thousands of people.

I remember the good and plentiful years of my early childhood: My uncles always bringing interesting people home from the University of Michigan to expose me to differences in philosophy; my father providing us with a satisfying lifestyle because of a successful business. Then came the Great Depression! It changed our life and how we looked at life. I lived through those years and was forever impacted by them.

Two events for some reason always seemed detached and not part of my chronological memory: participation in combat in World War II and to strangely return home as a different, but grown man. The other involved my profession, which put me in a position of actually touching and being touched by two race riots – one in Detroit and one in Baltimore.

I've had the opportunity to do many worthwhile things such as:

•Helping to create the way the voluntary sector raises funds to support its services – the United Way.

•With a partner creating a new voluntary charitable mechanism, now popularly called a Support Foundation.

•Participated in setting up systems to identify, recruit and train young men and women as professional and as lay leaders.

•Aiding the movement and absorption of the ingathering in the new State of Israel.

In addition, I had the unbelievable opportunity to help save one of the greatest universities of the world.

One of the principles I learned early in my career is that I'm involved in a volunteer system. For this system to perpetuate itself, volunteers must be in the forefront and they must receive credit. This account, however, takes us behind the scenes and discloses how many of the decisions and actions were really made.

There is a great deal to be written, and it is because of that I have undertaken writing it down. Good fortune smiled upon me when I met my publisher. He just said, "Start writing and keep going" – I have done as he advised.

ACKNOWLEDGEMENTS

I hope this memoir is informative for my readers and has special meaning to my family.

Cindy Hiller, Neal Kaye, and Howard Kleinman

Donald and Jacqueline Hiller

Jenny Niederriter, and Lilli and True

Danielle Schuman Olivier, and Tavi and Izzi

Warren and Marquita Wepman

Dr. David Kreisberg, Dr. Daniel Schuman,

Dr. Barry and Debra, and Andrea Wepman

My appreciation to my publisher, David Jordan

Thanks to my secretary, Kathie Carr

INTRODUCTION

In the fifty years, 1949-1999, addressed in this memoir there has been a number of organization changes. In 1999, the Council of Jewish Federations and Welfare Funds and United Jewish Appeal merged and became United Jewish Communities. In 2009, the organization was renamed Jewish Federations of North America.

The Associated Jewish Charities and Welfare Fund of Baltimore was recently renamed the Associated: Jewish Community Federation of Baltimore.

In this memoir, I have used the original names as they were at the time of the events being described, in order to make such activities historically correct.

To assist the reader, the following is a list of acronyms of frequently mentioned organizations.

American Jewish Joint Distribution Committee (JDC)
Associated Jewish Charities and Welfare Fund Baltimore (AJCWF)
Community Chests and Councils of America (CCC)
Council of Jewish Federations and Welfare Funds (CJF)
Jewish Agency for Israel (JAFI)
Jewish Community Federation of Cleveland (JCF)
Northwest Baltimore Corp. (NWBC)
United Israel Appeal (UIA)
United Jewish Appeal (UJA)
Jewish Community Federation of Pittsburgh (UJF)

N avigator to pilot; "we are two hours from home - over and out." It is so peaceful over the Atlantic. There is nothing in any direction. As the navigator, I had all the time in the world to think before we landed at a New England Air Force base.

This journey started on May 16, 1945, when I headed with my B-24 Liberator crew to Fez, Morocco. We were taking our plane, *Iron Gate*, in route for a checkup and then to fly her home. But V E Day, May 8th, changed it all. We left the *Iron Gate* and were ordered to fly back to the U.S.A. in a new B-24. We departed May 27th.

Our flight plan had us stopping in the Azores, Labrador, and Newfoundland and landing in the U.S.A. That was June 6th. All that time gave me a chance to think.

I had a complete and full tour, over 25 missions, with many of the most difficult targets - Ploesti Oil Fields, Prague, Vienna, and Munich.

I thought about Fred DeMatteis, my bombardier, who left one day to fly with another crew and was shot down. I wrote to his mother every day telling her that I was convinced he would be saved and would return. With the help of partisans he got back to our base and was sent home and discharged. He became a prominent New York builder, having built the apartment complex over the Museum of Modern Art in Manhattan.

I remember about how I screamed directions to Owen Serkus, our nose gunner, to take a picture of our squad leader, Colonel Morgan as he was being shot down. I am told that the photograph is in the Virginia Aviation Museum in Richmond, Virginia, according to Neil November, creator of the museum.

On my return from a mission to our Italian airbase on April 12, 1945, my ground crew told me as I stepped off the plane that President Roosevelt had died. I asked who replaced him. They said they thought it was a guy named Truman.

The sun was still shining and things were going through my mind, *How did I get here?*

As an Air Force reservist, I was ordered out of the University of Michigan at the beginning of my final semester, January, 1944. I was sent by train from Detroit to Miami for basic training. In Miami I was one of many thousands of enlisted men. I remembered my cousin, Ed Wepman, a Lieutenant Commander in the Navy, taking me to the famous restaurant, Joe's Stone Crab, which was off limits to enlisted personnel. I also will never forget Gordon McCrae who later became a Broadway and movie star, who was my physical training buddy and became a good friend.

From Miami I was sent to study astronomy and trigonometry at Erskine College in Due West, South Carolina; to Nashville, Tennessee, for classification; to Ellington Field, Texas, for navigational training; to Laredo, Texas, for gunnery and finally to Selma, Louisiana, for advanced navigation training.

Following my completion of navigation training and becoming a second lieutenant navigator, I was put together with a crew that was trained in the Savannah, Georgia, area. When we were finished with training, we were sent to Massachusetts for our final preparation for overseas combat. They gave us the week off which we spent in New York City. Owen Serkus' uncle, Jack Kreindler, who together with Charlie Berne, owned 21 Brands and the 21 Club, took us under their wings for a week in New York. Each night they gave us a different host, Ted Husing, Orson Welles, and Ethel Merman. The uncle footed the bills for all of our dining and entertainment. On our last night in Manhattan they presented us with the logo of the 21 Club (the Iron Gate) and told us that they would love to have our plane named the "Iron Gate." As a final goodwill gesture, they urged us to empty our footlockers. They filled each footlocker with Ballantine Scotch, which they knew was like gold overseas.

I remember heading to Virginia for departure and boarding a troop transport ship that would take us to Africa and Italy. That was my first cruise, can you believe, on a liberty ship? We docked in Oran, then to Foggia, Italy, the 15th Air Force, where we were installed in the 464th Bomb Group, 787th Squadron. There I was looking at a squadron of B-24 Liberators.

I thought back to the University of Michigan, where in the summer of 1943, in order to make enough money to pay my tuition, I drove a Coca Cola© truck. My biggest and most productive stop was in the Willow Run Ford Plant in Ypsilanti, Michigan. This is where the B-24 Liberators were assembled. At that moment, in Italy, I realized that I would be flying my old friends from Willow Run.

I recall my graduation from South High School in Grand Rapids, Michigan, where, of all things, I was granted the American Legion Award as the outstanding student. I actually had to laugh at the fact that I was now going to have the chance to join the American Legion since I lived through that tour of duty. My high school days were exciting and I ended as President of the School Student Council. When you are flying over the Atlantic, and all responsibilities are under control, once forgotten things come to mind. I actually visualized my tennis partner, Paul Sauerman, winning the Class A high school doubles tennis championship. That led me to think about pre-high school and I thought back to the days of the depression.

I will never forget as long as I live seeing our 1929 Essex put up on blocks in our garage because we couldn't afford to buy a gallon of gasoline. I thought about my poor dad who lost his business. I distinctly remember my mother's admonition as she sent my brother Don, age 6, and me, age 9, to the Heckman Cookie Factory to buy a bag of broken cookies and to stop at the creamery on the way home for a gallon jug of skim milk. Even though the depression looms in my mind, my mother's activities, probably among the greatest influences upon me, were unbelievable. Though there was very little money in our household, she ended up as President of the State of Michigan PTA, State President of the League Of Women Voters and Regional President and National Board Member of Hadassah.

I never had time to really think about how my parents coped during those very difficult Depression days. Sitting there at my navigation desk with the sun shining on our flight, I truly had time to cover some of the things that had never been put together in my mind. My parents were, in a sense, pioneers or at least in my mind they came from pioneer stock. My mother's father, Benjamin Wepman, had come to this country in 1890 and with a wagon and a horse had traveled from Detroit, Michigan, up into the hunting and Indian territory of Northern

Michigan. In 1893, he sold his wagon and his horse and bought a little house on what would now be the outskirts of Traverse City, Michigan. I was told that the reason he bought this house across from an Indian reservation was that he would be able to open up a small general store on the first floor. Well, this slight, five-foot-five-inch man bought a four-foot-long shotgun that he hung over the cash register so that nobody would attack him. My son, Josh, inherited that shotgun from one of my mother's brothers and he displays it with honor.

My mother was born in 1895, in Copemich, Michigan, the Traverse City suburb that no longer exists. In the middle 1920's my mother's family had migrated to Grand Rapids, Michigan, and in the 1930's, after my grandmother died, my grandfather and my mother's sister moved into our small three-bedroom house. My father remodeled an upstairs bathroom, making a five-by-eight space for Aunt Flo. Perhaps the fact that we lived through the Depression was based upon necessity and by our hearty pioneer background.

Back to the flight task at hand, I took another fix with my navigational instruments. I then saw that we were only one half-hour away from the U.S.A. I remember telling the crew to get ready for landing and gave the landing instructions to the pilot. Then I told him I was turning off my equipment. This trip was coming to its exciting conclusion.

We landed. We all went directly to the telephones. I will never forget reaching my mother and telling her that I was home on American soil, safe and sound. After all the excitement and the tears, she asked me if it were possible to get home quickly. My cousin, Ed Wepman, was being married on June 9th. He had been hoping I would be his best man. I now had seven days from that moment to get there. I told her that I would be there within 48 hours. I was able to get an Air Force flight to Detroit and a commercial flight to Grand Rapids. True to my word, in 48 hours I walked off the commercial airline. I looked for whoever was there to meet me. At the bottom of the steps, I saw this absolutely magnificent woman who had on a naval officer's uniform and looked like the Wave Advertisement. I said, "Who are you?" "I am Helen and you're coming to my wedding." I must have had my mouth open because I had not seen a woman this beautiful since my visit in New York where Ethel Merman had taken us to dinner and the show at Lou Walters Latin Quarter.

Circa 1928, Don and Bob, the Hiller Brothers, with Father Bill and Mother Anne

Marianne (top)   Helen (bottom)

Top L – Lt. Navigator 15th Air Force, Foggia, Italy, B-24 Liberator, *The Iron Gate*
Top R – Cadet Hiller, Ellington Field, Texas
Bottom, Cadet Hiller, Pre-flight Training

Wh-----hen I think about the most important day in my life, June 3, 1945, stands alone. My new cousin-to-be by marriage, Helen, and my cousin, Dorothy Rill, Ed Wepman's sister, embraced me as I deplaned from a Capitol Airways plane. After kisses and proper introductions, they drove us to Dorothy's home in East Grand Rapids, Michigan, where my mother and father engulfed me with hugs, kisses and tears. The living room was full of family and new family-to-be. I met Helen's mother and father. I was introduced to Marianne, her sister. It is not difficult to recall my feelings and emotions. Helen was a beauty. Marianne was a totally different, ethereal, woman – blonde, blue eyed, feather bobbed hair and the body of a pinup girl. My god, how could two sisters be so breathtaking? Never in the past 66 years, or in the 24 years before that, had I been so totally smitten by any person. When I talk about dreams that come true, it is usually an illusionary idea. This was real! It was coming true. This vision was life changing. I have re-lived that moment hundreds of times. It always comes out the same.

I tried to spend every moment of the next six days with Marianne. Even though I may have been an embarrassment to both families, I had this opportunity and I was not going to miss it.

By the time of Ed and Helen's wedding, I knew Marianne quite well, but not well enough. The Air Force had reassigned me to Atlantic City, New Jersey, for arrival on June 12, "for rest and rehabilitation." Marianne and I concocted a plan to be together. Marianne's mother's first cousin, Gertrude Friedman and her husband, world famous astrophysicist, Herbert, had a small cottage about 15 minutes drive from Atlantic City. Marianne convinced Gertrude to develop a plan that was acceptable to her parents, which had Marianne presumably moving in with Gertrude in mid-June. Without going into the details, Gertrude was not actually there, but we were. So, for nearly two full months, we were together night and day. We were in love and nothing could stop us.

Marianne was entering her senior year at Richmond Professional Institute, the art school of the College of William and Mary, located in Richmond, Virginia. Our plan was for us to be married in June, 1946. I was most likely to be reassigned and retrained in B-29s for Pacific duty. Two big events changed our plans. First, that guy Truman, by now my personal hero, brought the war to a close in mid-August. Part of our plan could now be acted upon. I was discharged in early September and once again placed in the Air Force Reserve. We thought we then had smooth flying.

On Thanksgiving morning I received a call from Marianne who was having family dinner in Virginia. She was on the phone in tears. Her two aunts — one from Norfolk and one from Richmond — had been aggressively telling her not to get married — especially not to "a poor boy with not a particularly great future." It may have been sound advice but not to two strong people in love. My response was "let's move the wedding up and not wait until June." So we picked the date of March 9. At the Thanksgiving dinner, Marianne announced to her family that we would be married and they were invited.

Much had to transpire. With her mother and father's help, they planned the wedding. We were married on March 9, 1946, at the Park Central Hotel in Manhattan.

I had secured a job as a veteran's counselor but now I had to develop a career plan. I consulted with a number of people. With my father's assistance I went to Milwaukee and met individually with each of his three brothers, my uncles – Harry Hiller, corporate attorney; Irving Robert Hiller, M.D., Chief of Surgery at Sinai Hospital; Samuel Hiller, M.D., internist in private practice. They all insisted that my first step after my wedding was to decide on my educational future. My two doctor uncles offered to pay all of my expenses beyond the GI Bill if I went to medical school.

Using my mother's voluntary career as a model, I spoke to a number of educators and successful community leaders. The consensus was that "community work" seemed to fit my interests and potential skills.

Three or four graduate schools led the list of the best schools in community work. My alma mater, University of Michigan's Institute of Social Work had, in my opinion, the best course because of Professor Arthur Dunham, who was the head of that specialization. I met Professor Dunham and we immediately bonded. He offered me a student job as his administrative assistant, if I would enroll at the University of Michigan, which was centered in Detroit, Michigan. After talking with the other two top schools, I viewed the Dunham offer as a real opportunity. The move to Detroit was a great offer and a career defining opportunity.

As Arthur Dunham's assistant I edited the *Journal for Community Organization* and he insisted that my name appear as the editor. I learned later on that this was a very prestigious position that he had held for several years. I completed the two-year masters' graduate course in 19 months, graduating first in the class; was elected to *Phi Kappa Phi*; and received the Detroit Social Work Award. My master's thesis was published as a monograph by Community Chests and Councils of America.

While I was working around the clock, Marianne started what could have been a potentially great career. After six months of working as a salesperson at Saks Fifth Avenue, at the Detroit Fisher Center, she was moving into the job of Fashion Coordinator.

Three months prior to my graduation from the Institute of Social Work, I began job searching. The national associations, such as Community Chest and Councils of America, (CCC), Council of Jewish Federation and Welfare Funds (CJF) had personnel departments with whom I registered. CCC had a number of opportunities to offer me but CJF sent me a strange reply. Dr Benjamin Rosenberg, Director of Personnel, advised that they had too many veterans returning and that I should look elsewhere. I mention this only because within 24 months CJF was having serious personnel shortages. I saved the letter as a teaching tool. In 1979, thirty years later, having been induced to take the position of Executive Vice President of CJF, I read the letter to my assembled staff.

My first job opportunity came from the Metropolitan Detroit Community Chest. Bob McCrae, Executive Director, offered me the opportunity to join the staff as a campaign and community organization associate. I was advised that my annual salary would be $3,200. I took it and told Marianne that it was only the beginning. Some day with the right opportunity, I believed I would earn as much as $10,000. I reminded her that perhaps her two aunts were correct – I would never make a large income.

If you happen to have the proper credentials, being in the right place at the right time is a paradigm worth examining. This is what I call opportunity. It came to me within 3 months of beginning my professional career.

Though my Masters of Social Work (MSW) Degree was granted August 13, 1948, I was able to accept a position with the Community Chest Of Metropolitan Detroit in May because I had completed all of the work, including my thesis. I had done my social work fieldwork at the Community Chest and knew the staff and the agency. When I started my new position I moved right into the Campaign Department headed by Walter Laidlaw, whose Associate Director, Richard (Dick) Booth, supervised me. Walter and Dick knew me well from my four months of work as a student.

Once I got unpacked and settled, Walter and Dick invited me to join them in a private meeting. Walter Laidlaw came from a business background and had been the professional brains and leader of the Michigan Republican Party. He knew all of the major corporate and business leadership of the state. Dick was a graduate of the Ohio State University School of Social Work and was a skilled professional who had worked for several years with Walter. They told me that they had asked Bob McCrae to offer me the position. They believed with my background, training, and personality that I could be their partner.

They were visionaries who saw that the Community Chest was not growing because of competition from five or six highly publicized national agencies. They had developed a plan to revitalize the Community Chest and they had designed an experimental program to test the plan. I was being offered the opportunity to join them. I thought taking the position in Detroit was my first professional opportunity. I then quickly learned that there were opportunities and there were **OPPORTUNITIES**. But I also learned that there were decisions and **DECISIONS**. I made my DECISION. It served as the jumping off point for my whole career.

Walter and Dick had designed a brilliant plan, but to implement it would require not only skill but also nerve. We put together a test campaign for a limited number of corporations including the ten largest in the metropolitan area. We would call the campaign United Foundation Of Metropolitan Detroit and it would include all of the Community Chest agencies, plus named diseases – heart, cancer, etc. A careful distinction was made not to name national agencies, but rather only the disease for which funds would be used. The only major national cause missing was the American Red Cross.

There were three fronts that had to be covered. The first was the campaign by corporations and their employees. The second was finding and/or creating disease-serving agencies that would participate. Finally, a public relations program had to be designed to educate not only the donors but also the general public.

Without my telling the full story, which Walter Laidlaw did in his extensive writing, I can say the experiment worked and was incorporated in the following year's campaign – The United Foundation of Metropolitan Detroit, community wide campaign, the first United Way!

Several aspects of the experiment in which I personally played a key role are informative. My first task was to get the Chevrolet Division, the largest and most influential of general Motors, to participate. I called on the President of General Motors, Charles E. Wilson. Oh yes, he later became the much-publicized Secretary of Defense of President Eisenhower's Cabinet. After just two meetings, he agreed to participation, if we could get the United Auto Workers (UAW) to agree.

My second task was to work with another specialized staff member to get Victor Reuther, who headed the community relations part of the UAW, to get union participation.

My third undertaking was to get Joe Parker, Assistant Treasurer of J. L. Hudson Co., to not only bring the Webber family of J. L. Hudson into this strategy but to be willing to use the company's name and prestige to help convince other employers.

One of the most important and interesting aspects of bringing together a united agency/cause constituency was Laidlaw's skilled handling of The March of Dimes and ultimately the American Red Cross, both of which had been under the direction of Basil O'Connor. O'Connor was without peer as a national cause fundraiser. But Laidlaw persisted and ultimately succeeded for the United Foundation of Metropolitan Detroit. This was the model and beginning of the United Way movement – a historic beginning. To be a party to Walter's thinking, planning, and execution was a unique learning experience for a 27-year-old professional.

In the first full United Foundation campaign I met and worked with a young and talented volunteer, Max Fisher, who was to become a major leader in not only all aspects of Detroit community life, but also in national and international Jewish organizational life. I remember a small birthday party given for Max by a group of leading professionals more than three decades after having worked with him in Detroit. He looked around the room, pointed his finger at me and acknowledged our long history. I mention this because in 1979-1981, I again worked even more closely with Max.

1948-49 was a period of great excitement for Marianne and me. Our first child, Karen, was born in August, 1949. I had taken Marianne to a Detroit Tiger baseball game and purposely had her walk with me to the upper deck to help induce labor. It worked. We made it to the entrance of Women's Hospital and Karen was delivered en route to the operating room. Yes, we had left the game in the sixth inning.

Election eve 1948, however, is a date that Marianne and I frequently recall. We had invited Dick Booth to dinner since his wife was visiting her family out of town. After dinner, we watched the election results on our new 12-inch Magnavox TV. Dick, an outspoken Republican, left about 9:30 p.m. because it appeared that Dewey would win. When he left, we two Democrats let out a mighty yell because that guy Truman was inching his way to victory. We stayed up until he was elected.

In the summer of 1950, we were planning the third United Foundation campaign and I needed some rest. My mother joined Marianne and me to help with baby Karen. We had booked a full week at Ludington on the beach at Lake Michigan. By midweek, I was beginning to unwind until the cottage manager brought me a message about a long distance call. The call was from Cleveland, Ohio, from Henry L. Zucker. I knew the name but couldn't understand why he would be calling. He had been the Planning Director of the Welfare Federation, which was Cleveland's council of social agencies (planning partner of the Cleveland Community Chest.) I remember his name from my days as Editor of the Journal of Community Organization. I assumed he wanted me to come to Cleveland to speak about the new United Way. Our experiment had been such a huge success we had many calls for speaking engagements.

I called Henry L. Zucker and learned that he was now the Executive Director of the Jewish Community Federation of Cleveland. (JCF) He told me that he was elevated to the position over a year ago, having been the associate for two years. He wanted to meet with me as soon as possible because he thought we might find a mutually beneficial working relationship. He told me that he had been seeking Arthur Dunham's advice, and Dunham had told him to pursue me. He also knew all about my United Foundation experience.

I drove my family back to Detroit and went to Cleveland to meet with Zucker. He was eleven years my senior and was a graduate of Case Western Reserve School of Social Work. He had spent his entire career in Cleveland. His campaign director was leaving and he wanted to bring someone on staff that could play a larger role than just directing the annual campaign.

There I was, after three years before being told by the Council of Jewish Federations and Welfare Funds (CJF) that there were no positions available. Then I was being offered the position of Associate Director of one of the principal Jewish Federations of North American. What intrigued me was not only working in the Jewish Federation field, but the opportunity to work with Henry L. Zucker. I could tell from just our meetings together that he was destined to become a national leader and someone from whom I could learn. He told me he sought me out because he believed that I could bring a new dimension to the Jewish Community Federation Of Cleveland (JCF).

I had been moving up rapidly in the United Way community and had to examine Zucker's proposal with great care. I felt I was ready for the more sober lifestyle of the Jewish community and what I had perceived as the personal passion of its community workers. After consultation and research about this opportunity, I made the decision to accept Cleveland's offer and move as soon as possible before the end of 1950.

The five years I spent in Cleveland were tremendously productive. One of the early actions I undertook was to help create and install the first computerized campaign system in the Jewish community. We did this by working with IBM programmers and actually running a duplicate program alongside of our manual system. This advancement is in itself a major story. Working with Rudy Walter, Finance Director, David Frieman, Comptroller, Mae Spector, Office Manager, Henry Zucker and I built a program that not only served Cleveland but also served a number of other communities as a computer campaign center.

The annual campaign structure was reorganized and the number of volunteer workers was substantially increased. This new model served the community for several decades. This was accomplished by developing leadership, the essential component to successful fund raising.

We structured a young men's leadership program, 25-40 years of age, and enlisted successful business and professional men in a one-year course. These men, whose names became synonymous with Cleveland's leadership, led the community for two decades. Since the program was new, I wrote and spoke about it at several national forums of the CJF. Each class was for a year of intensive programming with 10 to 15 participants. My final class, 1954-55, included a young business executive, Morton L. Mandel, who joined me three decades later as the illustrious President of the CJF, when I became Executive Vice President.

My Mentor, Henry L. Zucker, (Hank), gave me an enormous number of assignments in addition to directing the annual fund raising campaign. These assignments developed experience and understanding available to no one else in the field. Perhaps the most important axiom I learned was that we were involved in a volunteer organization and the volunteer had to be in the forefront with the opportunity for satisfaction. Hank also pioneered the development of endowment funds, which served as the model for me. That became one of my areas of innovation and achievement. In this area, Hank and I had some disagreement in later years.

I had been working with Rabbi Abba Hillel Silver on several major gift solicitations. So Hank had no qualms about asking me to travel with Rabbi Silver to the 1953-54 United Jewish Appeal (UJA) National Conference in Atlantic City. To understand what was to unfold, the reader should understand the agency relationships in the local - national fund raising structure, and comprehend the historic nature of Rabbi Silver's trip to this conference. This is essential in grasping the historic perspective of this event.

In as a brief and succinct form as possible the following is a limited description of the agency relationship in fund raising for overseas service in the 1950's through 1990.

Fund raising was the responsibility of 229 organized local communities that operate a locally governed structure, generally called a Jewish federation. It combines fund raising, coordination of services, planning, and budgeting. It had a national association of all federations known as CJF. This body was the national coordinating, convening, advice and guidance provider, but was not involved specifically in fund raising. (See Flow Chart on P.27)

The local Jewish Federations raised funds for local services, national agencies, and international organizations. The international organizations generally received more than 50 percent of the funds raised by the local community. The international agencies (overseas services) were represented by an organization that the two principal overseas agencies had created. The principals were American Jewish Joint Distribution Committee, (JDC), which provided services and funds to aid people in need worldwide, but not in Israel. The United Israel Appeal (UIA) represented and acted on behalf of the Jewish Agency for Israel (JAFI), which provided funds for immigration, rehabilitation, and absorption in Israel. The two organizations together created and constituted the United Jewish Appeal (UJA).

JEWISH FEDERATIONS FUND RAISING AND DISTRIBUTION FOR OVERSEAS SERVICES

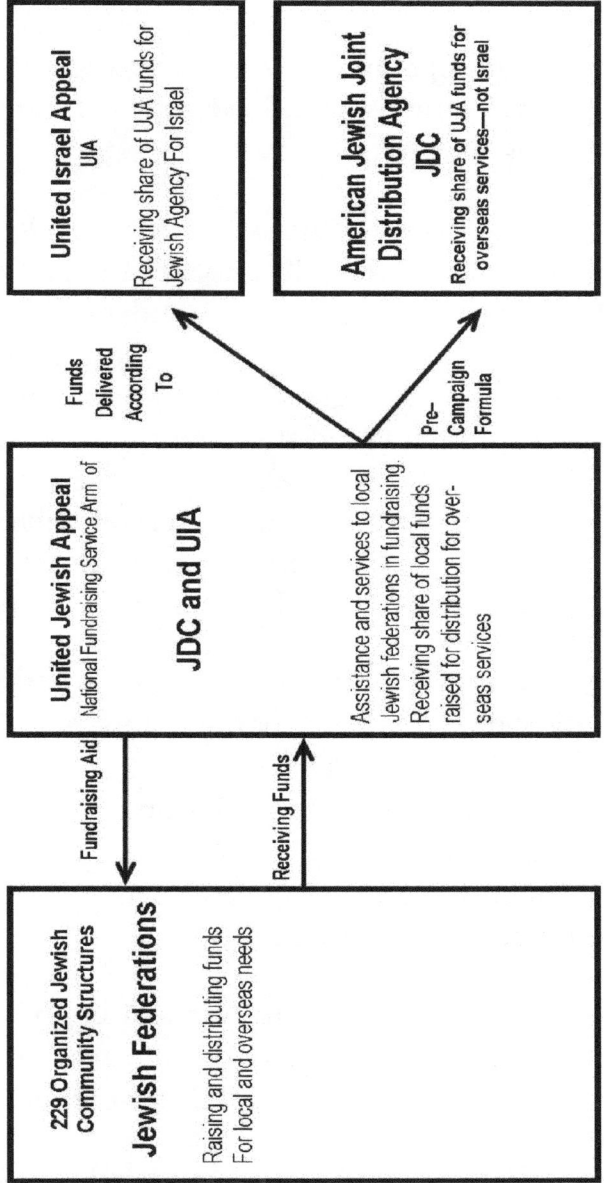

229 Organized Jewish Community Structures

Jewish Federations

Raising and distributing funds
For local and overseas needs

Fundraising Aid →

Receiving Funds →

United Jewish Appeal
National Fundraising Service Arm of

JDC and UIA

Assistance and services to local
Jewish federations in fundraising.
Receiving share of local funds
raised for distribution for overseas services

Funds Delivered According To →

Pre–Campaign Formula →

United Israel Appeal
UIA

Receiving share of UJA funds for
Jewish Agency For Israel

American Jewish Joint Distribution Agency
JDC

Receiving share of UJA funds for
overseas services—not Israel

The UJA was the national organization that provided fund raising services and leadership for the local community campaigns. It was the recipient of the funds that the local campaigns raised and transmitted to overseas services.

Looking at Rabbi Silver was like looking at a deity — over 6 ft. 2 in. tall, shocking gray hair that stood up and covered his large and handsome head. Wherever I went with him, people came up to him just to be able to say that they had greeted the great Jewish leader. Rabbi Silver had delivered the historic address on May 8, 1947, before the United Nations urging the establishment of the State of Israel. Most observers believe that this address mobilized President Harry Truman to take leadership in pushing the United Nations to act on Israel's statehood.

Rabbi Silver was one of the two recognized international leaders on behalf of Israel. The other was David Ben Gurion. They were on opposite philosophical sides of the Jewish people's relationship to Israel. David Ben Gurion won a complex political battle. Silver was forced to resign from the JAFI and was excluded from the UJA and its conference in 1949.

Silver had carefully repaired relationships during the ensuing five years and was invited to return to the UJA and to appear at its 1953-54 conference in Atlantic City.

Here I was, a 32-year-old professional, joining the great leader on his return. We enjoyed our lengthy train trip to Philadelphia and on to Atlantic City. We talked at length and I told him about my family. I explained to him that my new second daughter, Barbara, was born on December 10, 1952, and because of that, I had to miss my first UJA conference. Poor Barbara, from that year on I missed her birthdays because I had to be at the annual conference. He told me about his family, his wonderful wife and his son Danny, who I subsequently would get to know well.

When we stepped into the large ballroom of the hotel in Atlantic City, it was packed with more than 2,000 people. Rabbi Silver was introduced and for a full ten minutes he was greeted with a standing ovation. During his thirty plus minute address tears were rolling down my cheeks, the same as everyone else, as we witnessed the rebirth of a great man.

Immediately after the meeting adjourned, friends and admirers urged Silver to join them for dinner. However, the two of us snuck off to a little Romanian restaurant a couple of blocks behind our hotel. Mr. Chomsky, the owner, greeted the Rabbi by name when we entered. Old friends having dinner together. Few of the Rabbi's admirers really understood how he loved interesting people and good food, but that he always used his celebrity when it was needed. When we were in New York City together, at another time, he wanted to eat at Lindy's, the famous delicatessen. The waiting line stretched out to the street. We walked inside and he was immediately seen by the *maitre d.* He was warmly greeted and we were seated in a booth at once.

In the 1950's, the UJA held a major fund raising meeting in Miami Beach, Florida, during the winter season. I would spend a week in advance of this meeting talking with Cleveland contributors who wintered or vacationed in South Florida. The reason I did this is that the most skilled solicitor I've ever observed wanted me to be with him. Leonard Ratner, one of Cleveland's greatest philanthropists, and I would call on every major contributor from Cleveland. Our objective was to get their contribution or to ensure their attendance at the star featured UJA fund raising meeting.

On the occasion of the 1955 meeting, Rabbi Herbert Friedman, who was a Reformed Rabbi from Milwaukee and who served as the volunteer chairman of the UJA Rabbinic Council asked for an appointment with me. We met in the lobby of the hotel for several hours. He had been asked to be the Executive Vice Chairman of the UJA, the top professional position. I shared with him my view of the offer and advised about what I saw as the benefits and the pitfalls. He took the position in early 1955 and served with distinction until 1982. The actual pitfalls that I had described to him unfortunately came true. Those had to do with his inability to maintain a marriage with the demands of the position.

My first visit to Israel was in 1953. I made more than twenty such visits, taking contributors on fund raising missions. It was very difficult work but so very rewarding, not only in fund raising results, but also in the many Israeli friends that I made. The UJA made all of the arrangements. After Rabbi Friedman took over in the 1950s, the UJA assistance became much more productive.

On that first visit I had an unusual experience in the King David Hotel, in the men's room. I walked up to the urinal next to the newly appointed Chief Of Staff of the Israel Defense Forces (IDF), Moshe Dyan, who wore a patch over his blind left eye. We were both performing our necessary function. I introduced myself to him and jokingly asked him a ridiculous question relative to urinating with the blind left eye. He broke out in laughter and we talked for at least an additional five minutes. We became friends and I saw him frequently on my many visits to Israel. Since he was a serious collector of biblical artifacts, he invited me on one visit to his "home museum." I have several pieces of antiquity from his collection, which were gifts and purchases.

Professor Yigal Yadin, the great archeologist and the leader of the expedition that uncovered Masada, became a dear friend of Marianne and me. He took us on a personal tour of Masada. We kept in regular communication with him when he was a general in the IDF, but most particularly when he had political disappointments.

It was not only the great, but the interesting that I met in Israel. For example, Zev Vilnay, who trained all the great Israeli guides and wrote the original guidebook. Peter Jennings, when he was reporting from Israel and many other well-known reporters who ate and drank at Finks' Bar in Jerusalem. The press hung out at Finks enjoying the company and the best Hungarian Goulash in Israel.

My Cleveland experience encompassed only five years but the learning was beyond chronological measurement.

It was here that I learned the factions and the frictions of the Jewish community. Cleveland was a microcosm example from the very simple ethnic challenges – German Jewish vs. Russian Jewish; etc.; Zionist vs. non-Zionist; Jewish Defense Agencies - American Jewish Committee vs. American Jewish Congress vs. Anti Defamation League. And yes, Orthodox challenging Reform, through such battles as Jewish Federation's support of day schools or serving of kosher meals at Federation functions. The important lesson I learned from these differences was that through the Jewish Federation the community came together in a common cause. I had lengthy discussions with Zucker on all of these and other issues which became the most valuable background for a life of professional service in the Jewish community.

In the fall of 1955, Hank closeted me for several hours. He had been offered the executive directorship of one of the largest federations. He had been discussing this with the President of the Cleveland Jewish Federation. They had agreed that if he took this position I would be offered his position in Cleveland. I was about to turn 34 years old. All of the executives of the Big 16 communities were at least ten years older.

The Big 16 was an informal grouping of the 16 largest communities in North America. The executives met regularly at least once a year for discussions of critical concern. It was somewhat like a caucus for learning but not for action.

Hank turned down this offer and my daydream subsided – for about 3 weeks. He came to me in the week of my 34th birthday, with what he considered a lifetime opportunity.

One of the Big 16 communities was actually going bankrupt. The lay and professional leadership appeared incapable of pulling it together. He had done a bit of investigation into the situation. Hank and several of his Big 16 colleagues, together with Philip Bernstein, Executive Vice President of CJF had come to the conclusion that the community, Pittsburgh, Pennsylvania, was salvable with certain provisos. They believed that I should take on this challenge. I thanked him for his faith in me and somewhat sarcastically for my 34th birthday present.

I carefully explained this situation and offer to Marianne who had to be concerned about our little family of Karen, age 6, and Barbara, age 3.

I agreed to spend a week in Pittsburgh and to respond by the end of the week. I found a large number of impossible conditions and situations. The current executive director had been forced to resign and his senior associate was now the acting director. The staff, including the acting director, was totally immobilized. It appeared that the Federation would not be able to meet its financial obligations after ninety days. No Pittsburgh leader was willing to take on the responsibility. I was willing to consider it, however, because I envisioned a pathway to achieving recovery. I laid out my plan to Hank and he agreed that it could work. I explained it carefully to Marianne, pointing out all of the pitfalls and negative conditions. I told her that this was an opportunity. There was no precedent for it, but I believed that it could be done. So, with opportunity comes decision, but only after further examination and contemplation. If she agreed, we would be off to Pittsburgh. I told her I could be like my grandfather in his horse and wagon, contemplating going to the unknown in Northern Michigan.

Left – Rabbi Abba Hillel Silver, Chairs Cleveland JCF dinner honoring Bob Hiller. L-R Rabbi Silver, Bob Hiller, Marianne Hiller

Henry L. Zucker is congratulated by Morton L. Mandel of Cleveland JCF "Two in Our Generation Tribute," 1975 (Photograph Credit: Copyright Photo courtesy of Mort Tucker Photography, Cleveland, Ohio)

Bob Hiller greets PM David Ben Gurion in Israel, 1952.

General Moshe Dayan and Bob Hiller at breakfast in Jerusalem, 1977.

L – R: Bob Hiller, Professor General Yigal Yadin and Rabbi Herbert Friedman. Hiller thanks the professor for the private trip to Masada.

PM Golda Meir welcomes Bob Hiller to her office, 1969.

T hank you for seeing me. I am Bob Hiller and I appreciate you giving me an hour of your time, Louis." He responded, "Mr. Caplan." Just two weeks before I had met with Senator Robert Taft and it was "Bob." So be it. From that day forward it was "Mr. Caplan."

Mr. Caplan sat at his huge desk looking at me, a 6 foot 3 inch giant. He was about 5 foot 3 inches, a stern face, with the corners of his mouth turned down. I took a deep breath and explained that I was exploring the possibility of becoming the new Executive Director of the United Jewish Federation of Pittsburgh (UJF). I wished to share some thoughts for his guidance. He immediately jumped in with a disparaging characterization of the recently re-signed executive director.

In my mind I said, *Caplan, I know a bit about you.* I thought to myself that his circumstances reminded me of a Cleveland leader, Maurice Saltzman. Both had been orphaned as very young boys, with Saltzman growing up at Bellefaire, the Jewish Orphan Home of Cleveland. He was a graduate of my first Young Leadership Class, and was on his way to becoming a "zillionaire." With the corners of his mouth turned up, he would become a great leader in Cleveland. Caplan had been orphaned as a young boy in a small Pennsylvania town and had been taken to Pittsburgh, where he grew up. By his sheer brilliance and personal drive, he had become one of the premier Pennsylvania lawyers and among his group of clients were several of the wealthiest Jewish leaders.

I explained to him that I was convinced he probably was the only individual who could save the Jewish community of Pittsburgh from collapse. For the next forty minutes, I carefully outlined for him how this might be accomplished.

In essence, I would require two years of his leadership as the President of the United Jewish Federation of Pittsburgh. (UJF), during which time we would create a new face and reputation for UJF; recruit and train new leadership; put a physical face on the organization; make it the "place to be" and substantially increase the fund development.

I told him that I had just met with the Executive Vice President of the new United Way, which had come into being several months earlier. This executive knew me by reputation. He was anxious to work with me and welcomed me to Pittsburgh.

As I came to the end of my hour, I began putting my belongings together and said to my host, "well Mr. Caplan, you'll never get another chance like this. I think we need each other. I'm prepared to do whatever is required. What can I say to you on behalf of your community?" He smiled for the first time in our hour.

He said, "How do I know I can trust you?" I told him to pick up his phone and call Joseph M. Berne in Cleveland. I was sure he knew Mr. Berne since they were both national leaders of the American Jewish Committee. Joe Berne had no idea of my meeting with Caplan, however, I urged Caplan to call and get his opinion. He told his secretary to make the call. Within a minute, he had Mr. Berne on the line. Caplan walked into his private conference room. I spent the next ten minutes going over my notes, guessing about the outcome of that call.

When he returned he said, "Okay, I'll be on board with you. As soon as you make up your mind let me know." I told him that with his commitment I would make up my mind within 48 hours and get back to him. It was clear that we were going to be working together, so within 48 hours I made the decision to accept the Pittsburgh position.

It was the end of September 1955 and I had to complete Cleveland's 1956 campaign plan and make sure that all the leadership was ready to go. I had to go to Pittsburgh to find a home for my family; move the family and get started with the Pittsburgh salvage job. It was a huge undertaking, but with Hank Zucker's help and Marianne's encouragement, as well as her acceptance of more than her share of responsibility, we made the move.

Before I even start the tale of the Pittsburgh revitalization, I have to mention that seven months after the move Marianne and I returned to Cleveland for one night to accept the thanks from about 1500 volunteers gathered at the Hollenden Hotel Ballroom. My dear friend Rabbi Silver chaired the event and was in great form – telling all kinds of tales about me. He ended up reminding the gathering with great glee that it was in this ballroom that I had performed a "miracle" in changing ham to steak. Quite simply the hotel had erred and began serving chicken supreme, breast of chicken over a slice of ham. As soon as I found out I got the manager to replace the dish with steaks which he had to defrost, cook and serve.

So the "miracle man" of Cleveland would now have to perform several miracles in Pittsburgh.

As I explained to Mr. Caplan, we had to put together the 1956 campaign organization; mobilize the volunteers; and get at least two astounding large lead gifts to set a pace. Leon Falk and Harry Epstein, who could make the two lead gifts, were his clients. I knew this from my secret weapons advising me, Louis J. Reizenstein and Herman Fineberg – more about them later.

Falk was the 55-year-old steel industrialist who was viewed as the wealthiest and most influential Jewish leader in Pittsburgh. He was totally disinterested in the Jewish Federation. Louis Caplan and I visited him; got him to double his previous gift; and to agree to take on several other assignments. Epstein agreed to do the same.

Falk and Epstein met with us and we agreed that they would try to enroll Samuel Frankel, who owned his own insurance brokerage company, to serve as Campaign Chairman. Frankel was overwhelmed by the meeting but he took on the assignment. The campaign had a new level and in four months was successfully completed.

The volunteers were greatly excited and most agreed to join the next year's campaign, including Samuel Frankel, the Chairman.

Next year's campaign would be more difficult because we would require at least two, or more likely three, lead gifts to establish an increased level for giving. Knowing this, all during that initial campaign, I was searching for next year's models. Fortunately, I found them and was able to cultivate three new lead gifts. We would be ready to utilize them in setting the level and pace for the 1957 campaign. Without taking the time to tell about how we came to these three giants, other than to say that Sam Frankel gave me the clue, each of them require appropriate mention.

Charles Rosenbloom was the remaining member of a wealthy family that had made its fortune in liquor manufacturing. He was retired and not physically well. His financial guide and assistant, Mr. Goldberg, a very nice person but Rosenbloom's protector, was a barrier I had to cultivate. Charles lived in a beautiful mansion and was surrounded by beauty. His wife, Lucille, had been the internationally famous harpist for the Pittsburgh symphony and was not and had no reason to be interested in the Jewish community. Charles himself and his family had given support to overseas Jewish needs during the period in which Israel became a state. Their contribution had slipped back to a low level. Since Leon Falk and Louis Caplan were highly competitive with Charles, I took it upon myself to secure his support. Finally, with Mr. Goldberg's assistance, Charles grasped the Pittsburgh

Jewish community's situation and was prepared to make the contribution that we needed.

At the same time, I began working with the father of one of the members of my Young Leadership Group. Samuel Horelick was a brilliant engineer who had several working inventions and together with his partner had created the Pennsylvania Transformer Company. My good fortune was that at exactly at the time we needed Sam he was selling his business to McGraw Electric Company. Sam had a big heart. I knew he and his family would now become leading philanthropists. He stepped up beyond my hope to give our second campaign a huge gift and a great start.

The third candidate was a romantic character, Attorney Ben Paul Brasley. He was single and lived with only his help on an enormous farm north of Pittsburgh. I was lucky that he graduated from the University of Michigan Law School in 1906. We were a lot different in age but we were fellow alumni of the University of Michigan. He was not only a charming man but also wanted to do interesting things. He was an able and successful lawyer and businessman. He quickly stepped up to make the third large gift for our 1957 campaign. He also introduced me to Jonas Salk, who had been at the University of Michigan, but in 1947 moved to the University of Pittsburgh. Fortunately, Salk never connected me to the United Way in Detroit. Walter Laidlaw had taken on Basil O'Connor, who led the March Of Dimes raising funds to fight polio. He had been President Franklin D. Roosevelt's legal partner and had become President of the National Foundation for Infantile Paralysis. He and Salk did a great deal of work together. Brasley created a very successful business on his farm to aid Salk. He grew and developed all of the white mice that Salk used in experimentation. It was the white mice that led me to meet Jonas Salk. He introduced me to his wife Donna. She was a social worker by training and a very good friend of Mrs. Louis J. Reizenstein, Florence. These two women opened my eyes to true advocacy. Both were greatly honored for their work. Florence became a legend in the Commonwealth of Pennsylvania. But alas, shortly after I departed Pittsburgh, Jonas divorced Donna.

The physician in our leadership training was Sidney N. Busis, M.D, a local and national leader in otolaryngology. He was approximately my age when he joined my training group. His father, David, was my intrepid volunteer assistant who spent a part of every day doing anything and everything that time would not permit me to do. Dr. Busis truly emerged as a leader in many areas of his profession and in philanthropy.

It should be noted that Tibby, Saul Weisberg, my comptroller's wife, was my secret in-house weapon. She was an artist and created all of our invitations and printed materials, saving us thousands of dollars in art and printing fees.

During that four-month period, after my first campaign was completed, I was able, with Louis Caplan's assistance, to work out an allocation payment plan that would meet our agencies minimum requirement and would be within our new allocation budget.

I explained to Louis Caplan that we had to get a new presence. We had to move out of the expensive, but inadequate Community Chest Building in downtown Pittsburgh. I found land one block from our Montifore Hospital, in the Oakland section. This was where the University of Pittsburgh, the cultural agencies, even the ballpark was located. It was also just a short distance from the Squirrel Hill Section of Pittsburgh, which housed approximately sixty percent of our constituency. How we bought the land and built a modern functional building (it still exists today) is a story that has a number of interesting aspects. The one that always gives me a chuckle is my meeting with Julius Halpern, President and major stockholder of a Pittsburgh bank. I met with him and explained about the necessity of us having a fairly substantial line of credit. At the conclusion of my presentation, he said that since the United Jewish Federation was seeking such a large amount of credit that he would have to meet with his Loan Committee. I asked, "Who are the committee members." He responded, "I am." Of course, we got the line of credit.

During that same four-month period, I put together a Leadership Training Group similar to what I had done in Cleveland. Reizenstein and Fineberg assisted me in selecting and recruiting the best business and professional leaders it was possible to enroll. We were hopefully seeking 15 men to go through the one-year intensive training course. We got everyone that we asked.

Reizenstein and his wife Florence were respected community leaders. He was a past President of (UJF). Fineberg was a leader in B'nai B'rith, a national Jewish ganization. He agreed to succeed Louis Caplan as President, after Caplan's second year in office. Herman Fineberg remained a dear friend after we both retired in Florida.

The group of men in our training course was quite unusual. They served as the pool for two decades of leadership. Great names in Pittsburgh Jewish leadership were:

Rogal (Alvin)	National Insurance Company
Shapira (Saul)	Giant Eagle Food Chain
Levinson (Aaron)	Steel
Lowenthal (David)	Steel
Stark (William)	Uniform service
Ostrow (Gerald))	Uniform service
Rudolph (Leonard)	Restaurants and food chain
Cohen (Jesse)	Furniture Chain
Hamburg (Lester)	Appliance distributorship
Halpern (Bernard)	Banking
Latterman (Earl & Bernard)	Electrical equipment

Other leaders from Kaufman Department Stores, lawyers and a physician.

One day Herman Fineberg insisted that I meet a man younger than our leadership group, who he believed would become the outstanding leader of the Pittsburgh Jewish community. I met Don Robinson. Marianne and I took Don and Sylvia Robinson to Israel on a private first visit for them. True to Herman's prediction, Don not only became a great Pittsburgh leader and Chairman of the Board of JDC, but one of the most successful business-men in the community. Marianne and I see the Robin-sons' several times each winter when they visit their Flor-ida residence.

Pittsburgh was a great personal challenge. In fact, my physician taught me how to avoid ulcers, because in my first year the workload problems were so heavy I began to have physical reactions.

In Pittsburgh, I made two major policy decisions that were not sound, but from which I learned. Both had to do with advice sought by the Executive Director of the YMHA. He, Jerry Auberbach, had booked Pete Seger, singer and balladeer, who was at that time being accused of being a Communist. Jerry explained to me the pressure on him was great to cancel the concert. Instead of my en-couraging him to go ahead with the concert, I acquiesced and concurred with his decision to cancel it. About a year later, Jerry had been pushing his Board of Directors to allow him to open a sandwich shop restaurant in the YMHA. The Orthodox Jewish members objected because it would not be kosher. I did not urge him to make it kosher, and once again to go ahead with his plan. Both of these actions could have gotten a much wiser response from me. On several occasions later in my career, I made different decisions, which came from learning from these experiences.

With the successful fund raising, the move into a new building, and the large number of leaders recruited, our staff became invigorated. Jim Bronner, the Campaign Director began to be innovative and gave real leadership to the campaign organization. Saul Weisberg, our comptroller was able to work with our agencies because we were up to date in payments. He could also work successfully with our lay budgeting process. Mike Schwartz, our Planning Director, began to give planning leadership to our agencies. Mike and I both taught as adjuncts at the School Of Social Work, University of Pittsburgh. In fact, we collaborated on an article that I believe to this day is still in print. It describes how fund raising for social welfare services can employ the social work process of community organization.

I also worked closely with Dr. Cecil Shepps, Director of the University Of Pittsburgh School Of Public Health. The approach to community organization that I had utilized was very valuable to the public health field.

I had met Bernard Olshansky of the community wide Council of Social Agencies on several occasions when we were working on citywide projects. He was an impressive professional and I had inquired if he would consider working in the Jewish community. Shortly thereafter, I received a call from Hank Zucker asking if I could assist in recruiting a social planning professional for the Jewish Community Federation of Cleveland. This was my first opportunity to make a contribution to Cleveland. I made all of the arrangements and Olshansky left for his new position within three months. This was the first of several professional contributions I would make to Cleveland.

A most interesting personal story developed for me in Pittsburgh. My friend, Leon Falk and his wife Kathryn (Kitty) were divorced. She moved to Israel and bought a large home on the border in Jerusalem. She entertained many local and foreign dignitaries. My uncle, Irving Robert (now called Robert) left Milwaukee and resigned his surgical post after his wife died of cancer. He moved to Israel and became a dollar per year cancer research investigator at the Hadassah Hospital. I set up a date for him with Kitty. He was invited to her next party and met his future wife, not Kitty. Kitty introduced them and I now had an "Aunt Trudy," three years my senior. We became great friends over the years and still communicate.

In my later years in Pittsburgh, I was doing a good deal of consulting for JDC, and was doing a lot of speaking and writing for CJF. I had from time to time presented papers at our Big 16. The senior member of the Big 16, Harry Greenstein, Baltimore bachelor, and longtime executive of the Baltimore Jewish Federation, fell in love with my two daughters and my wife since I regularly brought them to our summer get-togethers. We were very close, but that was true with a number of the other executives. My third child, Josh, was born in Pittsburgh. So when he was five he joined us and met "Uncle Harry." At the next Big 16 meeting, Harry took me aside and pleaded with me to succeed him in Baltimore. He was not well and was not up to doing his work as he should. I thanked Harry for his confidence and told him I had received three other recent requests for meetings to consider new positions – Chicago, Boston and Los Angeles.

The visits to all three cities were worthwhile. The visit to Chicago was different and worth telling. The leadership in Chicago asked me to come for an interview and set a date in February. Marianne joined me on this trip. I was to meet the committee at noon at a private club. So before noon I took Marianne to the Art Institute of Chicago located on Michigan Ave. The wind from Lake Michigan was blowing so hard that there was a rope across the wide avenue, which we had to hang on to so that we could cross. When we got to the other side and I turned to go back, Marianne shouted, "If you take that job, I'm staying in Pittsburgh." By the way, a colleague of mine from a national agency took the position and he was succeeded by a young man still on the job today, and considered to be without peer, Steven B. Nasatir.

I had spent nine important and fulfilling years in Pittsburgh. Marianne and I had developed a large group of friends. Included in the group were two very bright women who I believed should become professionals. I urged them to get graduate training, which they did, and both earned advanced graduate degrees. One, Bea Ornitz, years later actually became the number two professional at the UJF. The other, Charlotte Davis, became an international consultant on large organizational systems. These two women, together with memories of my mother's skills, created a continuing pressure to urge women to seek important professional roles. I kept questioning the fact that only once in all of its history had a Big 16 community had a top woman professional and that had been in Canada with none in the United States

I also became heavily committed to the training of professionals for the Jewish federation field. I guided two young men, Don Gartner, and Larry Cohen, to take a training course that led to their graduation with MSW degrees. Both of them worked in the Jewish federation field.

It is impossible to even think about Pittsburgh and to pass over the greatest baseball game I ever saw. To understand the importance of this I want to share a bit of history. At the peak of the Great Depression, 1934, my father had actually saved enough money to take my brother Don, then ten years old, and me to Chicago. It was a special 13th birthday gift for me.

Prior to the Chicago trip most of the summer had been spent with my cousin Ed Wepman, sitting on our front porch and listening to the radio broadcast of baseball games. Since in Grand Rapids, Michigan, we were almost equal distance from Detroit and Chicago we had developed an American League favorite, Detroit Tigers, and a National League, St. Louis Cardinals. We were entranced by the "Gas House Gang," the nickname of the Cardinals. So, on our trip to Chicago we saw "the great one," Dizzy Dean and his brother Daffy win a double header from the Chicago Cubs.

The memory of that double header always had been my baseball highlight until the greatest game, which was in Pittsburgh in 1960.

My neighbor and dear friend, who was my son Josh's godfather, Herbert Rosenthal, had invited us to join him and his wife, Louisa at the final game of the World Series.

We sat in his box seats and watched Bill Mazeroski hit the famous homerun that defeated the New York Yankees 10 to 9. Though I played basketball and tennis, baseball always seemed to play a special role in my life. Just as I will never forget Mazeroski's home run, there would be other important baseball connections in my professional life.

Harry Greenstein, my dear friend and colleague, prevailed upon me to visit Baltimore. Quickly surveying the situation, I found that the Baltimore Jewish community was more than double the size of the Pittsburgh community. The funds raised in the last campaign, at a minimum, should have been at least double, but were actually only forty percent more. The volunteer involvement was substantially less. Though there was a large reservoir of leadership in Baltimore, only a few were involved.

But I had promised.

Chief Archeology Investigator demonstrating authentication process to Marianne Hiller and Herman Fineberg.

Marianne Hiller and Children's Village Director talk with children.

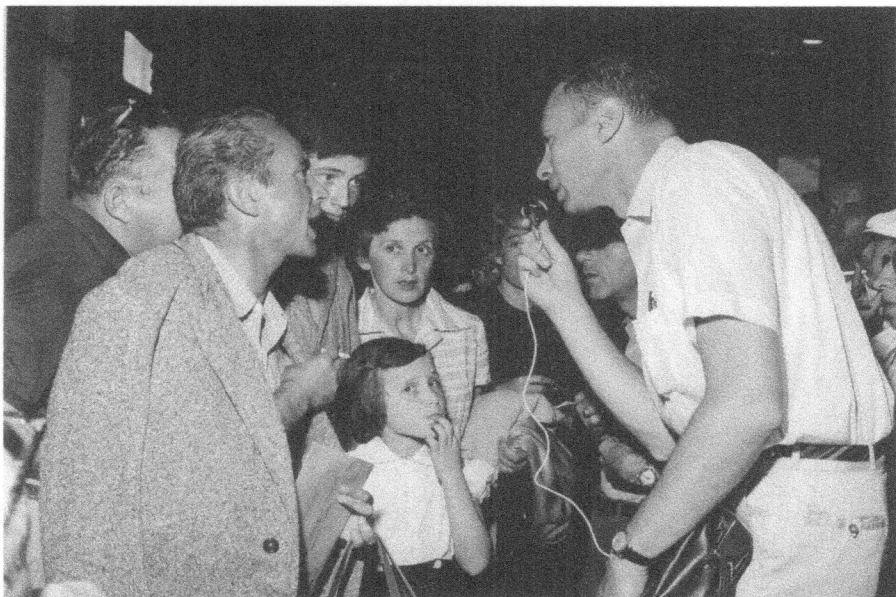

Bob Hiller talks with Russian arrivals at Ben Gurion Airport

1961 Mission – UJF President Lester Hamburg and Hiller at coastal installation near Caesarea.

**Waiting for visit with Israel President Ben Zvi at President's residence, 1960
L-R: Robert Hiller, Marianne Hiller, Rebecca Fineberg, Alex Robinson**

Pittsburgh and JDC leader Don Robinson and wife, Sylvia

Big 16 meeting, August, 1956, at San Diego. VIP visit to Submarine USS Raton by top federation executives and wives. Hiller's first of more than 20 Big 16 meetings. Fifth from right, first row, Isadore Sobeloft, Detroit. Behind him on the left is Marianne Hiller and on the right is Bob Hiller. "Official U. S. Navy Photo"

Robert Hiller and Professor Dr. Sam Haber. Professor Haber has reunion with former University of Michigan Student, now UJF Executive Vice President, Bob Hiller. Haber, representing ORT, speaks at UJF fund-raising meeting.

Baltimore's Associated Jewish Charities and Welfare Fund (AJCWF) Search Committee consisted of three distinguished leaders, all whom I knew. Louis J. Fox had just been elected President of AJCWF and was also Vice-President of the Council of Jewish Federations (CJF). Lester Levy was a past President of the AJCWF. Joseph Meyerhoff not only was a past President of the AJCWF but was the National Chairman of the United Jewish Appeal (UJA). It was an unusual meeting since the committee tried to convince me to come to Baltimore to assist them. They had included Harry Greenstein in the meeting that was held at the Southern Hotel.

The meeting was cordial, particularly since they asked me what I wanted or needed to take the executive director position. I explained that I would tell them my requests but most important was my bringing Marianne to Baltimore to see if this was the place we wanted to live. That was the early fall of 1964, and I was forty-three years old. I explained to them that if I took the position, I intended to remain until I was fifty-eight years of age. I said I had other plans after turning fifty-eight.

Marianne and I visited Baltimore in November and spent two full days looking at schools for our children and potential neighborhoods in which we might find the appropriate housing, as well as simply surveying the city.

I gave the Search Committee my wish list, which included a modest annual salary, but a supplementary retirement plan above the agency plan. We requested assistance in gaining admission for our three children to the Park School. We also required some assistance in finding suitable housing. The item that bewildered the committee was a request for two tickets for the NCAA Final Four College Basketball Tournament, which would be held in a couple of months at College Park, Maryland. The committee quickly agreed and we moved after the first of the year.

Associated Jewish Charities (AJC) had a sister agency, the Jewish Welfare Fund (JWF), which was the old model that had been discontinued by nearly all federations. They conducted a joint fund raising campaign.

We had to merge the two organizations to gain efficiency, and I suggested this to the officers of both organizations.

The headquarters was located in a fringe area of the downtown, Monument Street and Eutaw. The building was on the corner separated from a very large building by a parking lot. The large building had been the Jewish Community Center that was sold to a group of unions as a headquarters building. The AJC building was simply an office building with no amenities. I immediately recognized that it could be economically remodeled. If we moved the Women's Division to the Northwest Baltimore campus, it could give us space to create a small dining and meeting facility. The Women's Division welcomed this idea. The leadership looked forward to coming to the renovated headquarters for a salad or sandwich luncheon rather than an expensive and inconvenient hotel dining room. The food had to be kosher (my lesson learned), which was not difficult to accomplish, and which delighted a number of our leaders. This was accomplished in short order after my arrival.

The big issue, however, was one explained to me by Joseph Meyerhoff. It would require an educated and firm decision by me. I had just a few days to make a critical decision. The AJCWF had a series of buildings in Baltimore City on Park Heights Avenue, about two blocks before the intersection of North Parkway.

The buildings included a very sizeable Jewish Community Center; an office building that housed four agencies, plus the newly moved Women's Division. The third building housed the Baltimore Hebrew College and the Board of Jewish Education. Between and behind each building were excellent parking facilities.

Overview Map

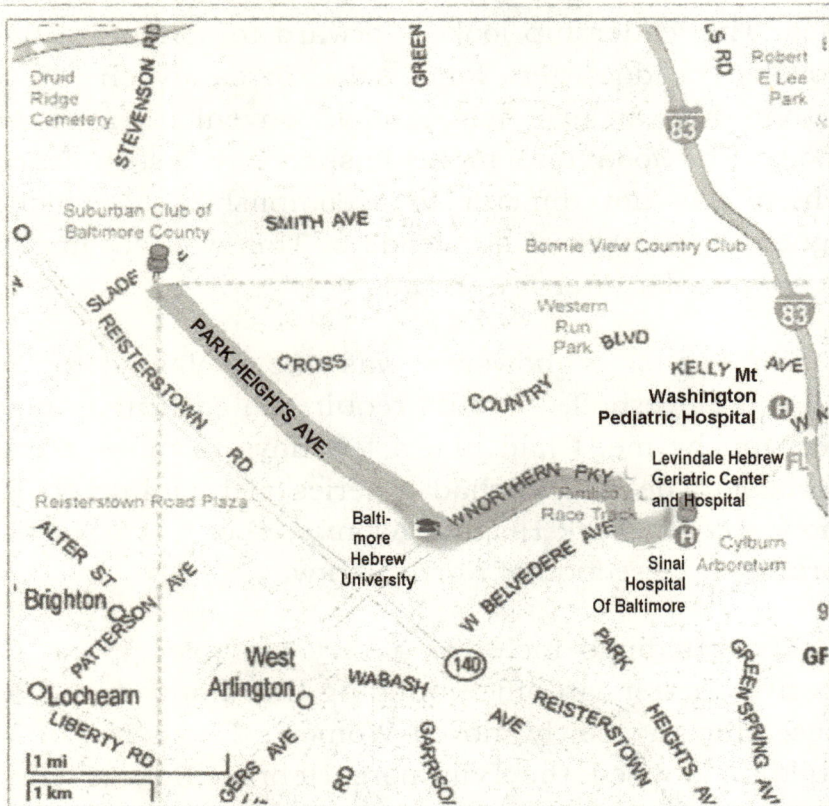

Joseph Meyerhoff, a builder and developer, said that he and several other leaders believed we should examine the idea of selling all of the Park Heights property and move to the suburbs. He pointed out to me that the Jewish population was moving in that direction. I suggested that I be given at least thirty days to give my reaction to any such plan. There's nothing like making a historic decision the first month on the job.

The first month in my new position was filled not only with the facility sale proposal, but it also required a decision on an urgent call from Philip Bernstein, Executive Vice-President of Council of Jewish Federations and Welfare Funds (CJF). The newly elected President of CJF, who had just taken office, was being forced to step down because of illness. Bernstein asked how traumatic it would be for me and for Baltimore if Louis Fox resigned as President of AJCWF and became the New President of CJF. I accepted the challenge and got Albert Hutzler, Jr., first Vice-President, who was next in line to succeed Louis Fox. New President; new executive; no more surprises.

Albert Hutzler and I started the process to get the merger completed and to complete the renovation of the office with dining facilities. I now had fewer than thirty days to reach my conclusion on the Park Heights facilities.

The decision I suggested would have enormous impact on Baltimore City as well as the Jewish community. I met with the mayor, Theodore McKelden, and his planning director. I also met with a number of synagogue leaders. Park Heights was known as *Rue de Shul* since there were three reformed temples and five Orthodox synagogues located on Park Heights from Northern Parkway north, two and a half miles.

South of Northern Parkway was a commercial and low income housing area, racially mixed and appearing to be in different levels of deterioration. This area included the famous Pimlico Race Track. A few blocks to the east of Pimlico were the two great health agencies of the AJCWF – Sinai Hospital and Levindale Home and Hospital for the

Aged. In addition was a plan for a senior residence adjacent to Levindale.

I met with Hutzler and Meyerhoff and gave them my conclusions, which they accepted and expressed appreciation. I told them I believed that it was very likely that we could sell the buildings and rebuild with very little additional cost. However, I believed the consequences could be disastrous. It was possible that the whole area surrounding the facilities would change rapidly and the neighborhoods would be destabilized. Religious facilities would probably have a variety of problems as a result.

I suggested that we should not sell. We should, however, upgrade all of the Park Heights facilities as required. But of greater importance, they should support me in developing a community organization with indigenous leadership serving a specific area both north and south of Northern Parkway. They accepted my recommendation, which actually put an end to the uneasy speculation. But, it also put another huge responsibility upon me.

Building a community organization to stabilize and strengthen an area was not impossible. This was to serve as the precursor of the Northwest Baltimore Corporation. Looking back it was clear that my first two months were filled with crucial considerations and actions; however, the basic activities of the AJCWF had to be revised and started.

The annual campaign required expansion and substantial upgrading. Fortunately, Isadore Sollod, the Campaign Director and his staff, were anxious to build with me. We had a number of top contributors ready to increase their gifts because they could see the community was in for revitalization. We also had a number of large contributors that needed very careful attention. There were several such contributors of note – one, a large contributor who needed his own kind of reassurance, and one a modest contributor who had the potential of becoming one the largest.

Jacob Blaustein was among the wealthiest 100 individuals in America. He was the largest stockholder of Standard Oil of Indiana. He was a past President of the American Jewish Committee, a national community relations organization to which he was totally devoted. We had a brief cordial introductory visit when I was giving consideration to taking the Baltimore position. Now I was about to meet him on the discussion of his contribution to our local campaign. I got through the amenities of our meeting and began to feel comfortable in the impressive surroundings. I recalled that over a decade earlier it was Blaustein who had worked out an actual "understanding" with David Ben Gurion that had sidelined my old friend, Rabbi Silver. Blaustein, like Henry Morgenthau, Jr. (President Roosevelt's Secretary of the Treasury and a UJA leader) were opposed to Silver's idea that world Jewry (Diaspora), would have a voice in the Jewish Agency for Israel governance. Blaustein, a non-Zionist, and Ben Gurion saw no reason for interference in the Zionist politics. Of course, I did not raise any part of my past relationship with Rabbi Silver. Blaustein, on the other hand, had actually looked forward to our meeting because he wanted to make sure Baltimore AJCWF would continue its high level of support for the American Jewish Committee. Once we got past that issue, he advised me what he would do for the campaign. On my departure, I was introduced to his son, Morton, who would pick up his mantle two years later.

The second prospect situation was far more complex, but ended up a few years later in a manner for which only an optimist like me could have wished. Aaron Straus built a chain of family and variety of stores, Reliable Stores, up and down the east coast. It had created and continued to create a fortune. A large portion of this fortune was regularly channeled into the Strauss Foundation. Straus, a generous man, was a follower of Rabbi Morris Lazaron, who was a leader of the American Council of Judaism. The American Council for Judaism was closely tied to the Classical Reform Movement and was actively anti-Zionist. They did not see an Israel as a Jewish homeland. The largest single supporter of this organization was Aaron Straus. This led to an interesting distribution of Straus Foundation funds. The Foundation made large gifts to the American Council for Judaism and a small token gift to the AJCWF campaign, about one-twentieth of what it could have been.

I began with Alfred Coplan, a young officer of Reliable Stores and a board member of its Foundation. He was an intelligent and thoughtful businessman. He could see the folly of the Foundation's actions. Fortunately, Rabbi Lazaron was retired by the Baltimore Hebrew Congregation and his successor, Rabbi Morris Lieberman, was a brilliant leader who not only supported the work of the AJCWF but also gave leadership to the annual campaign. Coplan, because of his ability, ultimately became the true leader of the Foundation. He also became a President of Baltimore Hebrew Congregation, but most importantly, he became President of the AJCWF. In a very short time, the Foundation became a major contributor to the AJCWF annual campaign. These two contributors – Blaustein and Straus – joined a group of other leaders who gave the annual campaign tremendous growth. Actually, including special fund raising for Israel emergencies, the annual campaign quadrupled in size in less than ten years.

I must indicate that the Baltimore Jewish community had a plethora of powerful people. Two unique leaders emerged when we conducted special Israel Emergency Fund Campaigns. Harvey (Bud) Joseph Meyerhoff led my initial Baltimore regular 1966 campaign. He worked and the community responded with exceedingly generous contributions. Just a few years later, Bud took on the task of leading and raising the funds for the Holocaust Memorial Museum in Washington, D.C. which he helped dedicate in April, 1973. He will forever be remembered for this leadership achievement.

In 1972, Jerrold (Chuck) Hoffberger agreed to lead the second special Israel Emergency Fund. This too was a huge fund raising success. Chuck went on to lead CJF as its President. He was asked to fill in for his brother-in-law, Irving Blum, who had to step aside because of ill health and then his passing away. Chuck ultimately became chairman of the Jewish Agency for Israel.

I single out these two cases because they played key emergency roles for the Baltimore Jewish community and then went on directly to high-level national and international responsibilities.

Harry Greenstein shows new executive, Robert I. Hiller, the AJCWF budget for 1966.

**The front of the AJCWF headquarters,
corner of Monument and Eutaw.**

**Hiller (L) and Joseph Meyerhoff discuss future
of Park Heights Facilities**

Louis J. Fox (L), President Associated Jewish Charities, 1965, was succeeded by Albert Hutler, Jr., ® two months after Hiller arrives.

Milestone Moment – Ground-Breaking for "The Concord" the AJC's first senior citizen apartments, March 1968. L-R: R. I. Hiller, Abe Kostick, Marvin Wahl, Melvyn T. Pugatch, Albert D. Hutzler, Jr. Leroy Hoffberger, Robert Weinberg, Eugene Feinblass, Lester S. Levy.

Within a week after my arrival in Baltimore, J. Jefferson Miller, an executive from the Hecht Co., called upon me. He was a leader of the Community Chest and pointed out that Baltimore was one of the few cities that had not yet created a United Fund. He knew my personal history and felt I could not only give him advice, but could also assist him in creating a United Way Campaign. I explained that I was not overwhelmed, but that I was stretched a little thin. I finally agreed that in a month I would meet with the leaders who were essential to making the United Way become a reality.

We met with the Community Chest lay and professional leadership and their legal counsel and the executives of the Catholic Charities. It was clear that Catholic Charities had many misgivings about the United Fund campaign. Based on the information given to me, I suggested two major changes. First, Associated Jewish Charities and Welfare Fund would give up its non-Jewish campaign and be included in the United Fund campaign for the amount currently being given to its non-Jewish campaign. The other suggestion was that Catholic Charities, which raised about eight times the amount of the AJCWF's non-Jewish campaign, would give up its campaign and be in the United Fund for that amount. If we could get agreement on these two basic principles, we could work out all the other details. It took us about three months and many meetings between the leadership of Catholic Charities and the United Fund. United Fund was made workable and after several rocky campaigns, and with executive change, it became a solid organ for the community.

I was invited to meet with Albert Berney, Chairman, and Parren Mitchell, who was the executive of Baltimore's new Anti-Poverty Program. Mitchell was previously chairman of the Maryland Human Relations Commission and later a long-term congressman. Parren and I became close friends and we worked on a number of projects. This meeting led to my having contact with a number of area and grassroots black leaders, several who became good friends and allies. I got their advice and cooperation on my proposed plan to develop an organization in Northwest Baltimore to improve the living conditions and to help give stability to the area.

Because of my work with Catholic Charities on the United Fund, Cardinal Shehan and his appointee, Monsignor Francis Stafford, who oversaw the work of the Catholic Charities, together with Hal Smith, the able executive director, believed that I could be helpful in a study and restructuring of the Catholic Charities. Dr. Ruth Young, Professor at the Maryland school of Social Work and its future dean, and I were asked to do a study. This took about five months and ended in a variety of administrative and functional changes. Because of this work, I had developed good working relationships with a number of individuals working in the inner city.

I had to get the Park Heights grassroots organization going as I promised when we determined to remain on Park Heights Avenue. Eugene Feinblatt agreed to be the Chairman of the Northwest Baltimore Corporation (NWBC). He was the senior partner in the law firm that had been headed by Simon Sobeloff, the former Solicitor General of the United States. Gene was also the volunteer assistant to Baltimore's Mayor Thomas D'allesandro, III. With help from a community worker in Philadelphia, who had done what I had hoped to do in Baltimore, we got a surprising number of local leaders involved. The best news, however, was that we were able to engage Margaret Pollard professionally as our executive director. She was a black woman, trained in community work, and respected by everyone who had the opportunity to work with her. She was as skillful as any worker with whom I had ever worked. She stayed with NWBC for the critical six years, from 1967-1973. In those years, the organization actually created a form of stability in the area. It enhanced the life of the local residents - gains were made in neighborhood cleanup and delivery of city services. Most important, several new services were created with resident involvement. The most successful new service was a community health service. Since Sinai Hospital was the largest institution in the area, and its outpatient department was the family doctor to most residents, long lines and long waits were commonplace. With the support and help of Sinai, Margaret Pollard and a small group of local residents, together with several skilled volunteer workers put together an outpatient clinic located in the middle of the Park Heights neighborhood. Samuel Frank, a leader of the AJCWF, aided by several skilled volunteers, took on the task of making the clinic work. It did work and it became the crown jewel of NWBC.

With Dr. Martin Luther King, Jr.'s death, racial unrest and rioting overtook both east and west downtown Baltimore. On April 6, 1968, Governor Spiro Agnew ordered the National Guard to quell the looting and fire setting. There was a curfew established and travel was restricted in and out of the city.

On April 9th, I got a call from Eugene Feinblatt asking me to bring a toothbrush and get down to the Mayor's Office, where he and Mayor Thomas D'allesandro, III, had been for the past two days. He gave me driving instructions. I drove through Druid Hill Park and gave my name to the National Guard officer, who allowed me to travel to city hall and park. I did not use the toothbrush because I came home at the end of a very demoralizing day. Our community's black leadership had been pushed by Governor Agnew to get them to condemn the rioters. What was needed was a cooperative action, not angry public comment. Finally, the Mayor had the respite he was looking for and it appeared that we would see a painful effort to get things back to some level of operation. But Agnew kept up the pressure, which many of us believed delayed the outcome by at least twenty-four hours.

I had been talking to northwest Baltimore black leadership who assured me that calm would remain in our area, but they told me that from lower Park Heights Avenue, all the way through the west side of Baltimore (passing by my office by less than a mile), was in shambles. I saw this a few days later when I was allowed to travel to part of the area.

The other thing I did was to talk to small neighborhood shopkeepers who were friends of the neighborhood and had served it. They could not understand why they were being looted or burned. We explained to them that there would be some kind of help as soon as things quieted down. I worked with the Hebrew Free Loan Association in getting them some kind of financial aid. This turned out to be a small number since many could not or would not start up in the area.

It is not possible to describe the debris and property devastation. Huge numbers of federal troops, National Guard, the Baltimore Police and Fire Departments, and city officials had finally quelled the storm.

The first riot I experienced was in the summer of 1949, in Detroit, Michigan. Compared to 1968, it seemed like a neighborhood upset. This Baltimore experience was indescribable and emblazoned in my mind forever. Mayor D'allesandro, III, his assistant, Kalman (Buzzy) Hettleman, Eugene Feinblatt and the other city officials were hidden heroes. But it was the very leadership that Governor Agnew criticized who worked tirelessly and was ultimately successful.

Though I was able to function from my home and from our Women's Division office in upper Park Heights Avenue, it took about a week to get back to my office.

Just prior to the riot period, Robert Levi, Hecht Co. executive, an individual who had given great service to the Baltimore community, got me involved in trying to get a fully operational Baltimore Community Foundation. Our ingenuous approach to having the Goldseker Foundation's Executive Director, Timothy Armbruster, take this task on as part of his duties, made it possible to finally have an operating Baltimore Community Foundation.

Tim and I worked together on this, but also on a number of other Baltimore projects. He was a great addition to the Baltimore non-profit scene.

Working in our Women's Division office for those few days once again raised the old question about women's role in the voluntary professional leadership of the Jewish community.

When my mother became a top volunteer leader in the State of Michigan, I was sixteen years of age. It was 1937, and we were just beginning to move on and out of the Great Depression. It was not unusual for me to believe that a woman could achieve any top level of leadership. However, I learned that mother was the exception and not the norm. I was bothered and it nagged me throughout my professional life. I had to be an advocate for women's leadership. It was not only part of the gene pool, but also an extended view of the model. This situation was unproductive and certainly unfair.

Though my several years in Baltimore were so packed and over packed with responsibility, I could not refuse the request to teach one course at the University of Maryland's School of Social Work. It was a course in advanced administration. In my opening session a small woman made absolutely sure that she sat directly in front of me. Her name was Barbara Mikulski. I'd been following her career from that day on and through her many years in the Senate. Even though Barbara is a senator, she always defers to me and introduces me as her professor. She made sure that I took the first step in front of her. Today as I watch her on television, I think back to that girl from the working class of east Baltimore, now giving top leadership in the United States Senate. Senator Mikulski reminds me that women could lead our system, but where have they been in my Jewish community system?

In 2009, Margaret Pollard passed away in Chapel Hill, North Carolina, at the age of seventy-seven. She had been NWBC's first full time executive, forty-two years earlier, at the age of thirty-five. The six years she served convinced me at the time that I would hear about her in the future. She was brilliant, skilled, and possessed a great sense of herself. I mention her at this point because she emerged as a leader in her community. For ten years, she was a Chatham County, North Carolina, Commissioner, and she was the first and only black woman to chair the Commission. I followed her career when she left Baltimore. She continued to give me inspiration; another woman reaching great heights. These examples proved that it was possible for women to achieve top leadership positions. Why not in our highly competitive Jewish community organization system?

I think back to Pittsburgh with two cases of lay leadership – Florence Reizenstein and Donna Salk. In addition there were two cases of professional leadership – Bea Ornitz and Charlotte Davis. These were great achievers, but not at the top of our Big 16 Jewish system. Those that I mentioned confirm that the possibility was there. I made up my mind that it was my responsibility to find the way. I could and should design and develop a plan to achieve this within the lay leadership of Baltimore.

Finally, I had the opportunity to work toward the objective. I made the decision to work at full throttle and to achieve it. The initial part of my plan had a very sad ending, but it was nearly a success. Peggy Pearlstone, Joseph Meyerhoff"s oldest child, had professional training and was a wife and a mother. She had been the President of the Jewish Family and Children's Service and had led the AJCWF Women's Division campaign. Bright, attractive, well liked and respected, Peggy was an ideal woman to work through the steps to becoming the first woman president of the AJCWF. She had the help of her husband, Jack, who wanted her to succeed. I discussed this in detail with Peggy and Jack and we were in total agreement to move forward. The initial steps getting her nominated as a first vice president of AJCWF and having her play a leadership role in the big gifts of the campaign were underway. Cancer became the obstacle that could not be overcome. It was a great loss to a great family and a heartbreaking loss for a grieving community. We urged Jack to step into Peggy's role, which he did, in her memory. He became an excellent president. Peggy and Jack's son, Richard, later became President of the AJCWF and the National Chairman of the UJA.

I had to start over. I had two other candidates – Shoshana Cardin and Barbara Himmelrich. Shoshana herself describes how she rose to top national and international leadership and how we planned her career. One crucial aspect not mentioned is that before each major step of her long career, we met with her husband, Jerome, and had his full support. She, as only she could, spells it out.

* "*I had the help of several mentors along the way – all men because at that time there were no women to whom I might have turned. Bob Hiller's effect on my life was quite direct. From our first meeting, when I refused to be pressured into merging the Federation of Jewish Women's Organizations with the Women's Division, of the Associated Jewish Charities, Bob quietly marked me as someone to be watched. He tested my skills when, as campaign co-chair of Women's Division, I suggested raising the level of giving among the women. After I passed that test by attracting women to participate at a higher level, Bob invited me to join the Associated's executive committee as a vice president. While there were further tests along the way, it was this step in particular that propelled my voluntary career into a higher orbit. When he moved to CJF, he quietly and without my knowledge, made certain I was tapped for various roles at CJF as well. Just a few years later, he was directly responsible for my advancement to the top leadership spot.*

At the same time, I was watching Bob and I was learning from him. He succeeded Harry Greenstein as director of the Associated Jewish Charities, an out-of-towner replacing a long-admired figure in the community. He quickly earned the respect of the Baltimore leadership with his quiet intelligence, political savvy, and commitment to the city. Bob was one who could put together a broad coalition to address a particular objective and then select the right professional to manage it. He could compromise with others, but knew when to insist that certain

standards be met. He was persuasive and prag-
matic and always in control, with the best interests
of the community uppermost in his mind. I took note
of his skills and expertise, lessons to be put to use
at the right moment. I even mimicked his largely ex-
temporaneous speaking style and found that it
worked well for me. I learned from Bob that a lead-
er needs to radiate poise and self-possession to
remain in control. When he validated my efforts to
do just that during the disruptive protest at the To-
ronto General Assembly in 1984, his approval pro-
vided me with a much needed boost in confidence. ”

*** Memoirs of Shoshana Shoubin Cardin, 2008 – Jewish Museum of Mary-
land, Baltimore, Maryland 21202, Pages 192-193.**

What gave me additional confidence in Shoshana is
the fact that she became President of the AJCWF after I
left Baltimore and President of the CJFWF and Chairman
of the board of the UIA after I was on to the next phase of
my career.

A somewhat different scenario emerged with Barbara
Himmelrich. She had enormous, but well guarded ambi-
tion. My advice to her was that she had to develop more
knowledge and additional skill. She took this seriously
and went to graduate school, getting a Masters of Social
Work from the School of Social Work, University of Maryland. Armed with new credentials, but more important,
new self-confidence, she made her way, with Sam, her
husband's help and support to the top spot as Chairman
of the Board of AJCWF. Her achievement also came after I
had left Baltimore.

Several other women may have sought upward movement. Clem Kaufman was a leader of the Women's Division, who had the capacity to serve in a higher office, but she opted to get a PhD at Johns Hopkins University and moved in the academic field. Gloria Harris was a skilled women's Division leader, but used her talents for other organizational activities. With Shoshana and Barbara leading the way, Suzanne Cohen, a young, recently widowed leader emerged as Chairman of the Board of the AJCWF. This was not my first-hand doing, but rather a legacy of my mission.

The other aspect of my vision was to recruit and to train new professionals for the Jewish community field of service.

**Peggy Pearlstone,
First Vice President AJCWF**

**Shoshana S. Cardin, First
Woman President AJCWF 1983**

**Barbara L. Himmelrich, Board
Chair in 1990's**

**Suzanne I. Cohen, Board
Chair in 1990's**

D r. Daniel Thurz, Dean, University of Maryland School of social work and Dr. Leivy Smolar, President of the Baltimore Hebrew University, presented me with what they termed a partial proposal. They believed that by creating a joint program between their two institutions, leading to a double master's degree, students would be better equipped to serve the Jewish community. I pointed out several major weakness and offered solutions. What emerged was the Baltimore Institute of Jewish Communal Service.

The primary focus would be to get top quality young men and women properly trained for Jewish community service. This would require a high caliber fieldwork experience, which would be given by AJCWF, the Wilmington Delaware Jewish Federation and appropriate national agencies. I took the responsibility to set up the fieldwork and to get the program certified by the CJF. This certification would bring with it access to scholarship funds.

Dr. Smolar agreed to hire top-level professors in the field of government and international relations. Dr. Robert Freedman was engaged also to play an administrative role in the program. The CJF was thrilled by this new development, which stimulated several other programs –

at Brandeis University and Hebrew Union College, Los Angeles, California

Our recruitment was even better than we had anticipated and the first several classes graduated real stars. We had several outstanding women – one became Executive Director of the Jack Pearlstone Center. Her name is Carole Pristoop and the other, Gail Chalew, is the Editor of the Journal of Jewish Communal Services. The men graduates included the future executive vice president of the Cleveland Jewish Federation, Stephen H. Hoffman, who also served for a period as executive vice president of CJF. One of the other interesting graduates was Larry Moses, whom I personally enticed at a later date to become the assistant to Rabbi Morris Corson, Executive Vice President of the Wexner Foundation. Larry ultimately became the executive vice president of the Foundation.

Just as in Cleveland and Pittsburgh, I developed not only a Young Men's Leadership Program, but in Baltimore, I also developed a Young Women's Leadership Program. Both added some new training facets to what I had previously done. The graduates of these programs formed the nucleus of leadership for years to come. One of the graduates joined me in later years in one of the most substantive decisions of my career. Just as Morton L. Mandel of Cleveland and I collaborated in CJF in New York in 1979, so did Morris W. Offit cooperate with me in 1992 on probably my most far-reaching decision. (This is the subject of Chapter Seventeen). Because of the nature of the decision, I will elaborate on it in detail later in this memoir.

Early in my Baltimore career, I engaged Carmi Schwartz to be the executive of our Women's Division. He was a well-trained and attractive social worker, originally from Montreal. He did such an outstanding job that by 1970 he was elevated to the position of Director of Social Planning. During the same time period, Martin Waxman was engaged as our Public Relations Director. He had been the public and community relations director of a union headquartered in Washington, D.C. In a short time Marty advanced to be Director of Fund Raising when Isadore Sollod stepped aside. With Louis Friedman, Director of Finance, these three professionals became the nucleus of our senior staff.

We undertook some innovative approaches to planning. Three particular undertakings were new to our field. We did the first professionally directed demographic study. This was followed by an area study combining the demographics to determine where the Jewish population would move in the decade to come. To accomplish this required cooperation from the county and state governments. They shared with us their road and various types of transportation projections. The outcome was definitive and led to early and bold action. We were actually able to pinpoint an area that was still not developed. The center of this area was on farmland owned by the former candidate for governor, George P. Mahoney, who lost to Spiro Agnew, in the gubernatorial election. I searched out, found his business manager, and began to negotiate to purchase the land. I then brought in Bernard Manekin, a leading realtor and a future president of AJCWF. I wanted to buy about 60 percent of this tract. Manekin and I ended the negotiation by purchasing 155 acres at approximately $3,000 an acre. By the time I brought the proposal to the Board of Directors of AJCWF, I had a contributor (Hugo and Helen Dalsheimer) willing to cover not only the land purchase, but also about two-thirds of the cost of a new youth center to be built on the land. The Board of Directors eagerly approved the purchase. I was able to get another family, a brother and two sisters – I. D. Shapiro and Mrs. Levinson and Mrs. Levin, to endow a summer camp facility adjacent to the proposed youth center. It gave me great satisfaction years later when Joseph Meyerhoff, II, the grandson of the previously acclaimed Joseph Meyerhoff, became the President of the Jewish Community Centers, which included these new facilities. He reminded his board that the purchase had been called by some; "Hiller's Folly." He told them that the unused one hundred acres (Fifty acres were now being used), was worth a minimum of $55,000 per acre. He later told me that I should have been in his business rather than in community business.

A second innovative study was done by my old friend and colleague, Dr. Cecil Shepps, who at that time was the founding director of the University's Health Services Research Center, University of North Carolina. As "University Professor" he had all the resources of the university at his call. He guided our study committee in a study of the needs of the elderly. The outcome of this set our plan for future services for the elderly for a decade in the future.

A third planning undertaking evolved from my dissatisfaction with what was called social planning. A word of history – when I came to Baltimore in 1965, no planning structure existed. All planning was done *ad hoc*. One of the first innovations I introduced was a year round planning structure handling planning and budgeting. There were approximately three hundred volunteers involved. It brought a new feeling of ownership to the contributors of the AJCWF. I always felt long range social planning was a misnomer. It really was strategic planning for agency service. I did extensive research and consulting on the planning process. From this, I was able to design and develop a long range planning system. That involved long-range (five years) goal setting and methodologies for attaining such goals. The key to the system was the annual review. Modifications were made each year based upon the actual achievements. It was a continually changing plan and new goals were established for five more years. I was able to further develop this type of continuous planning and it became part of the tools I used when I was involved in community studies in later years.

Another exceedingly successful undertaking was our financial investment plan. This had never been done by any Jewish federation.

After the merger of Associated Jewish Charities and Jewish Welfare Fund, we kept the corporate shell of AJC and used it as a subsidiary corporation to AJCWF. Its new mission was to develop and invest our endowment funds. Walter Rothchild was President of the AJC and he appointed Alfred Coplan to work with him on the new investment plan. After extensive interviewing of financial investment companies and investment advisors, we created a program that divided our endowment resources

sources into a series of specific types of investments. Each one of these groups had an individual counsel who was given total discretion to invest the account. All of the investment counsels were supervised by a single investment advisor. The results were annually reviewed and each investment counsel could be retained or dismissed, based upon comparisons to agreed-upon norms. This became so successful that individual investors pleaded with us to let them invest in our system. Of course, we could not do this. Other Jewish federations requested us to invest their endowment funds for a fee.

The new planning approaches had other signification ramifications. For example, in September 1972, Irving Blum, immediate past President of AJCWF and I were joined by four other top campaign leaders on a train trip from Baltimore to New York City. The six of us were to attend an emergency meeting convened by UJA to aid Israel. Israel was being attacked in what was historically called the "Yom Kippur War." I privately had told Blum that unless someone took leadership, the New York meeting would have little impact on the enormous national fund raising requirement. I suggested to him that we stand up at the beginning of the meeting and announce that without board authority we were taking it upon ourselves to pledge a one million dollar gift from our endowment fund (one million dollars was significant in 1972). Blum, a brilliant speaker, got permission from the other four leaders and dramatically made this announcement. It made the meeting! It elevated the level of emergency gifts to unprecedented amounts. Sidney Lansburgh, Jr., the new President of AJCWF, stepped in and gave distinguished leadership to the emergency campaign.

There are two key points to the incident. First, it established the fact that among the purposes of endowment funds was that they could be used in emergencies. Second, it demonstrated to all 229 Jewish federations that endowment funds were an essential component to federation financing. As an aside, this was my first difference on endowment funds with my old mentor, Henry L. Zucker. The other was that a specific amount, substantially less than the total yield of the fund, should be put into the annual resources for agency need. Hank and I debated this at several national meetings. My final answer always was that the more we constructively use a limited amount of income for our services, the more contributors would increase their endowment gifts.

Back in the 1960s, we began the process of merging the AJC and the JWF. Calman Zamoiski, Jr. (Bud Z) who was President of the JWF was the key leader in bringing organization into the merger. It wasn't until the end of 1969 that it was completed. Early in 1970, Bud Z, President of JWF, and Irving Blum President of AJC, celebrated the merger. Blum became the first President of the new AJCWF. I am positive that if Bud Z were asked about the most historically significant action he ever took he would not even remember his role in the merger.

Calman Zamoiski (Bud Z) led
Jewish Welfare Fund into
merger with Associated Jewish Charities creating AJCWF
– 1970.

Alfred Coplan – Chaired the committee
that developed the investment program
of AJC.

Walter Rothchild,
AJC President
(Sussman Photography,
Baltimore, MD)

L-R: Jacqueline Levine, V.P., CJF, Hiller Executive, V.P, and Blum, President, AJCWF. Congratulations from CJF on merger of AJC and JWF, 1970

Vice President Hubert H. Humphrey with Hiller to kick off 1969 campaign.

Blum and Hiller listen to Adlai Stevenson at camp kickoff, 1970.

**Martin Waxman Director Public Relations 1970,
elevated 1975 to Campaign Director**

In July 1975, I brought Steven Solender on to our staff. He replaced Carmi Schwartz, who left to become the Executive Vice President of Metropolitan New Jersey Jewish Federation. Steve had been in Europe as a senior JDC executive and was being courted by Big 16 communities to become a part of a local Jewish federation.

My colleague, Henry L. Zucker, was also courting Steve. When Steve saw what Baltimore was doing, he analyzed his opportunity for advancement and selected Baltimore. In just a few months after he became a part of the Baltimore staff, I was able to take on many new assignments both nationally and internationally. The Baltimore leadership believed that its executive should give such service as long as the home front continued to grow. This is why Baltimore was a great community. It saw its role, not just in Maryland, but as a part of a national and international social service system.

During this period, at Ralph Goldman, JDC Chief Executive's request, I made several studies for JDC – one in Italy regarding transmigration of Russian refugees and one in Morocco assessing it as a safe haven. I also did a part of a national study for the National Jewish Welfare Board, the central body of Jewish community centers.

These activities broadened not only my knowledge, but also my relationships with leaders worldwide.

At the time I arrived in Baltimore, the Baltimore Orioles, having been moved from St. Louis a decade earlier, were totally acquired and owned by my leadership and close friends. Jerrold (Chuck) Hoffberger became President and Zanvyl Krieger (Zan) was the largest individual stockholder. Chuck's box was behind the third base dugout and Zan's was just behind third base. How do I explain to a reader the dilemma I had my first year in Baltimore? Of course, Chuck and Zan invited the new executive to the World Series. I had seen Dizzy and Daffy Dean on my thirteenth birthday pitch a double header. I saw Bill Mazeroski hit the famous homerun that beat the Yankees in 1960. Now here I was alternating between the two best boxes in the stadium to watch the Orioles pull off one of the great upsets of baseball history. With Frank Robinson, the only Most Valuable Player in both leagues leading the way, the Orioles defeated the two greatest pitchers of the era. They beat Sandy Koufax and Don Drysdale by sweeping the series. It was game four that is etched in my memory: Frank Robinson's fourth-inning homerun, the only score of the game. Our Dave McNally and the Dodgers' Don Drysdale each gave up just four hits. More to come about baseball.

Chuck Hoffberger felt connected to me, so late in 1976 he asked me to come to New York to the offices of CJF. He had recently been elected President, and he knew the organization needed a complete overhaul. My advice to him was that we had to do a national study to see what the constituents (229 Jewish Federations) wanted and needed. Yes, they were unhappy, but what would give them the leadership and services that was required? I urged Chuck to get the very best lay leadership. He said he would if I would serve as the professional director of the study. I told him that I had a better idea. He should get Henry L. Zucker and me as co-directors. I urged him to get Ray Epstein, past President of CJF, Chicago, and Morton L. Mandel, of Cleveland, slated to be the next CJF President. I knew it suggested a "Lincolnesque" leadership. All three of these men believed that they knew the answers. It was a great tactical move – Ray, Chairman, Mort, Chairman of the Steering Committee, and Chuck, President. Hank and I, plus a group of young professional executives, kept the process on track. We built a consensus as we proceeded. The study concluded with a special assembly in Denver, Colorado, in 1978. The constituency gave it enthusiastic support.

Steven Solender and Robert Hiller. Solender joined AJCWF staff in 1975

Hiller accepts consulting and lecture requests with Solender's arrival.

L-R: 1st row (seated) Rabbi Y Y Ruderman, 2nd row, L-R, Solender, Grand Sephardic Rabbi of Israel, Leroy Hoffberger, Robert I. Hiller, at Ner Israel Yeshivot – 1979

First Blum Memorial Lectures
L-R: Robert I. Hiller, Phillip Bernstein, CJF, Lois Blum, son Larry and brother J. C. Hoffberger

CJF Study led by Jerrold Hoffberger, President, CJF, Raymond Epstein, Past President, CJF, and Morton Mandel, President Elect, CJF

L-R: Robert I. Hiller, Balimore AJCWF Executive and Henry L. Zucker, Cleveland JCF Executive. Zucker and Hiller served as co-directors of CJF Study. Epstein, Study Chair and Mandel, Chair of the Executive Committee of the Study.

In 1975 the annual campaign was flourishing under Martin Waxman's professional leadership and with our extensive development innovations of the past ten years coming to full maturity. This gave me time to devote to what I called a "the third leg" of the financing table, endowment development. The day I arrived in Baltimore I began a multi-faceted endowment development approach. It began with my predecessor Harry Greenstein and former AJCWF President Louis Fox waging an extensive "letter of intent" campaign. It was a simple moral agreement convincing a contributor to the annual campaign to commit himself to make an endowment fund contribution. This could be done either during his lifetime or through bequest.

When Harry passed away, I brought in new staff to lead a more comprehensive effort. The first director, George Kessler, was able to get the legal profession involved in our undertaking. We needed the attorneys' because they, among other things, were advisors to clients in estate planning. After George left, I hired an attorney who was working in the Jewish federation field, Joel M. Breitstein, as his successor. The program flourished and we began to have more reliance in our "Third Leg."

Because of my interest in endowments, I made contact with a former Cleveland attorney who had just recently retired as the Assistant Commissioner of Internal Revenue Service. He remained in Washington D.C. working with a prestigious Cleveland legal firm. His office was less than an hour from mine, so, former Internal Revenue Commissioner, Norman Sugarman and I renewed our Cleveland friendship.

Sugarman was becoming a national expert throughout the nonprofit field. We talked frequently and he shared with me an idea he was developing. It involved creation of a sub-corporation to an existing charity, which used the purpose clause of the charity. The public charity would select a majority of the trustees and the family creating the new support foundation would have minority membership. What he envisioned could give a donor a permanent connection to a public charity with a shared mission and the availability of all the charity's resources – professional staff, investment, etc. The support foundation could sustain family participation and charitable giving and could perpetuate the family name. In addition, there would be a tax benefit to the donor. There would also be a savings on excise taxes. This new concept needed a perfect family situation in order to have a proper model for the public to understand.

Sugarman's idea was in my mind but I had another serious problem to solve. AJCWF was becoming the "place to be," not only in the Jewish community but also in the general non-profit community. Our old home on Monument Avenue could not handle the volume of business and lay participation. Therefore, I began an approach to solving the situation. Once again, I put on my real estate hat and went to work.

I did my research and found what I believed was the prime location. It was less than a minute from the Jones Falls Expressway that served all of Baltimore as the north-south route. The location was right in the middle of a growing cultural center, which included the Maryland Institute of Art, University of Baltimore, Lyric Theatre and the future home being planned for the Baltimore Symphony Orchestra. The corner I wanted housed a discount catalog company, W. Bell and Company

I decided to pay a visit to the senior Mr. Bell. I introduced myself and said to him that according to my studies he ought to be selling me his building and moving to another location. He said to me, "you're crazy." I said, "No, Mr. Bell, I'm not crazy. This is the exact location that the Jewish community must have to remain in downtown Baltimore." Mr. Bell, who was not Jewish, caught his breath and said, "how much will you pay for it?" Now, this was a beat up old building with very limited parking. From my research I knew that adjacent to Bell's building was a parking garage that the city of Baltimore was going to lease to the Baltimore Symphony Orchestra (BSO). I recited the limitations of the building for Mr. Bell and said "how about five hundred thousand dollars?" He was about to get up, turned around and said to me "can you bring me a contract?" I told him I needed twenty four hours.

After an emergency meeting of the AJCWF Executive Committee, preceded by my having Bernard Manekin do a quick appraisal, we brought Mr. Bell a contract which Bernard Manekin had him execute.

"How much will it cost to build the building"? A member of the Executive Committee had inquired. Manekin quickly replied "a little more than a million." I suggested that the Executive Committee give me a week (what was entered in the contract). As an aside, within two weeks of our signing we were offered one million dollars for the property by the University of Baltimore.

Following the signing by Mr. Bell, I had past President Louis Fox in for a strategy session. I told him that I had my eye on Zanvyl Krieger (Zan). He was a very astute lawyer who always played second fiddle to his older brother. Zan was a creative man who had been the key visionary bringing both the Orioles and the Colts to Baltimore. He was a wealthy man, having substantial profits in real estate. Zan had reached out to me in my earliest days in Baltimore. In fact, I sat in his box at the World Series when the Orioles beat the Dodgers

Louis Fox made a lunch date with Zan for the next day. What transpired in the next forty-eight hours could be written as a one-act play or at least a New Yorker short story.

Zan owned the Lord Baltimore Hotel. So we were his lunch guests in the hotel dining room. We spent about fifty minutes of my outlining the need for a new home; its location and surroundings. I explained that we had an option on the property but we needed one million dollars. I told him we wanted one contributor to do it because we wanted to name the building the Zanvyl Krieger Community Building. He asked if he could take a look. We drove him to the property and he said he would give us an answer before noon the next day. He called the next morning and said that we had the one million dollars, but he wanted to make sure that the building was done attractively. So, if we needed another half million dollars he would make it available.

After advising the Executive Committee and the Board of the AJCWF, I immediately got in touch with Joseph Meyerhoff, President of the Baltimore Symphony Orchestra. At that time, I knew he needed temporary office quarters for the Baltimore Symphony Orchestra while its new facility was being built. We made a deal that he could use the Bell building for a year (giving us time to get plans, permits, etc.) In exchange he agreed to our use of the city owned BSO long-term parking garage lease without charge for as long as we needed it.

Zanvyl Krieger loved the process we went through and he kept talking to me about other possible projects. He told me the story of his recently acquired enormous wealth. Bill Veeck, the former owner of the Orioles, with whom Zan had worked to bring the team to Baltimore, had a home in the eastern shore of Maryland. Zan had received a call from Veeck, who asked him to do a favor and see a "sort of strange guy," who was pestering him to invest in a new company. Zan agreed and he made a date with Leon T. Hirsh. Hirsh had the patent rights to a Russian invention of a bone stapler which he claimed could be used in surgical proceedings. He needed money and he needed help from a nationally recognized surgeon to use and validate the procedure.

Zan liked Hirsh's idea and his aggressive approach, so he took a gamble. Dr. Mark Ravitch, a brilliant surgeon at Hopkins hospital became involved. Zan bought a huge number of shares of stock at pennies per share. He then became Chairman of the Board of the US Surgical Corporation (USS). At the time, Zan indicated that he had more than two hundred million dollars in USS stock. Of course, this tale has many interesting chapters of its own.

Zan's two children, both daughters – Betsy and Jean, were friends of my oldest daughter, Karen. In fact, Jean followed Karen to the University of Cincinnati. Karen was like an older sister all through college and beyond. The Krieger girls were very close to their mother Isabelle, but very distant from their father.

Norman Sugarman and I had the perfect model for the first "support foundation" Yes, in fact Zan was the absolute perfect candidate – a wealthy man wanting to be charitable, children with whom he wished to connect, and the nonprofit Corporation, AJCWF he trusted.

I met with Zan and then with Zan and Isabelle. He was interested and intrigued by the concept particularly that it had never been done before. Isabelle liked the charitable idea and the fact that her daughters could be involved. She saw this not as baseball or football, but as something meaningful for her family.

I met with Zan's attorney, Milton Schiller, managing partner of Weinberg and Green, the law firm of which Zan was *At Counsel,* and where he had his office. Milton was enthusiastic because of the concept and because he would have the opportunity of working with Norman Sugarman.

Norman came to Baltimore and met with Zan, Isabelle, Milton and me. He pointed out that when we proceeded he would have to get a Letter Ruling for a tax exemption from the Internal Revenue Service, since a 509 [a] 3 organization such as this would be a subsidiary to an approved 501[c] 3, the AJCWF. Further, this was required because there was no precedent.

We proceeded and all went as Norman had outlined. We had created the first "Support Foundation", the Isabelle and Zanvyl Krieger Fund (ZK Fund).

On July 28, 1978, the first Board of Directors met with Norman Sugarman. The family members were Isabelle, Betsy and Jean Krieger, and Dr. Herman Krieger Goldberg, Zan's nephew. By design, Zan was not a board member. I was elected President and Betsy and Jean, Vice Presidents. Louis J. Fox, Leroy Hoffberger (President elect of AJCWF), Bernard Manekin, President of AJCWF, and Milton Schiller were nominated by AJCWF to be the public members. There was the required one dollar in the ZK Fund's account. But by board acclimation it accepted Zan's contribution of one and a half million dollars to be its first grant. It was to the AJCWF to build the new building, the Associated Krieger Building.

Having already made history, there was one more endowment concept that I wanted to implement. Bud and Lyn Meyerhoff had four attractive and intelligent children, three girls and a boy. I knew them all and was impressed by their down to earth intelligence. I have previously, in this memoir, talked about Bud, but not about Lyn. She was a powerhouse. She was involved in the Republican Party and was on the Republican National Committee. She knew my political views and we frequently exchanged opinions. I will forever remember one hot summer's day on the Chesapeake Bay with Lyn and I sitting on the stern of their yacht, fishing and talking while everyone else was in the air-conditioned salon. I met with Bud and Lyn and outlined my suggestion. The Meyerhoff family already had a very sizable foundation with Dr. Louis Kaplan, renowned educator, as its director. My suggestion to them was to create a new Meyerhoff Foundation, with their children as the only trustees. It was essential to infuse the foundation with sufficient funds to make it interesting and worthwhile and to advise the children that there would be more funds coming in the future. They were enthusiastic about the idea and gave me permission to talk to their children.

Terry, Lee, Jill and Joseph, II, carefully explored the idea and agreed that it was something they would like to do. So, The Children of Harvey and Lyn Meyerhoff Philanthropic Fund was created. It worked so well that Lee became the star attraction at Jewish federation meetings throughout the country, explaining the benefits of the concept.

I had accomplished nearly all of my objectives for Baltimore and as I had advised the search committee on the day I was engaged, I planned to retire by my fifty-eighth birthday. That day was soon coming but as frequently happens – good plans are subject to change.

Organization Meeting of the Isabelle and Zanvyl Krieger Fund
L-R: Norman Sugarman, Former IRS Assistant Director, Betsy L. Krieger, VP, Dr. Herman Krieger Goldberg, Milton S. Schiller, VP/Secretary, Louis J. Fox, LeRoy E. Hoffberger, Jean Krieger Kahn, VP, Robert I. Hiller, President, Bernard Manekin, Treasurer
Seated: Isabelle Krieger, Board Member, Zanvyl Krieger, Benefactor, Non-board Member

Harvey and Lyn Meyerhoff together with children, L-R, Jill, Lee, Joseph, III, Terry, create first Children's Philanthropic Fund.

L-R: Robert Hiller, Samuel Himmelrich, Bernard Manekin. Hiller, ex VP, CJF, returns to Baltimore, Spring 1979, to congratulate campaign chairman Himmelrich and AJCWF President Manekin. Hiller had planned and started campaign in the fall of 1978.

Hiller's last visit to Israel before planned retirement, 1977, – visiting old friends and Mayor of Jerusalem, Teddy Kolleck.

L-R: Hiller and Professor Vilnay, author of *Official Israel Guidebook*.

I n preparation for my forthcoming planned retirement, I set in motion two undertakings.

One of my original ideas was that I would establish my own consulting firm that would feature consultation to nonprofit corporations. I had contacts throughout the country and believed that I could create a successful and profitable business. It was my plan to do this for approximately ten to twelve years.

The other idea was one that I had to convince Marianne to try. This was to establish our primary residence in Florida. Since our daughter Barbara and her family had moved to Florida, it appeared to me to be a logical plan. We implemented this undertaking first. Without going through the details, we bought a small home in Boca Raton, Florida.

I was winding down all of my professional responsibilities, and in fact was working with the President of AJCWF, Bernard Manekin and the executive committee to elevate Steven Solender, my assistant since 1975, to be my successor.

By now I should have known that opportunities appear when least expected. Decisions must be made.

The leadership of CJF asked me to join them at a meeting in New York in the spring of 1978, relative to the study that had been completed a few months earlier. At this meeting, President elect Morton L. Mandel, and the current President, Chuck Hoffberger, and Philip Bernstein, Executive Vice President spelled it out to me. They believed that I was the only professional that could implement the study and lead the CJF. Bernstein pleadingly said that he was not the person and that everyone knew it would take my professional ability to do this. I immediately advanced my arguments about my retirement and my business plans, and explained that the pressure they were putting on me was not reasonable. So, here it was: the decision that had to be made. Was I willing to change my plan of fifteen years? Would I accept the challenge to lead our national organization? I said I would need at least a week to consider this request.

During that week of consideration, I had an executive committee meeting of the AJCWF previously scheduled. My friends at CJF had talked to Bernard Manekin so that my own executive committee urged me to take what they kept calling the "top job."

Marianne suggested that if I did not take the job I would probably always have regrets. It would be difficult for her but she would, as always, give me her full support. So, my new career and retirement plan would be delayed for two more years.

I met with the CJF committee and they agreed to my conditions, which included a two-year nonrenewable contract. They accepted responsibility to employ my successor, with my assistance. The financial aspects were limited and reasonable.

We moved to New York but kept the new town house we had purchased in Baltimore when we sold our home. We now owned our new Florida home, a townhouse in Baltimore and were about to rent a Manhattan apartment for two years. I felt like I was in the real estate business.

CJF offices were on Lexington Avenue, directly behind the Waldorf Astoria. On my first day I began the unpacking ordeal and the determination of what would be hung and what would go into storage.

I had pictures of every Israeli Prime Minister from David Ben Gurion to Menachem Begin. I would have many more with Begin because he was the current Prime Minister. My favorite picture, however, (it was to be hung) was taken in Washington, D.C. at a gala party where Marianne and I were with the then Ambassador, Yitzhak Rabin, and his wife, Leah. Since we were close to Washington, D.C. we joined him at several events during his five years there.

Another photograph that made me reminisce was one of former Cleveland leader, Ezra Shapiro. He and his wife, Sylvia were both not only Cleveland leaders, but Zionist leaders in the United States of America. The picture I had was taken in Jerusalem where they had moved in the early 1970s, when he became the International Chairman of the World Zionist Organization (Karen Hayesod). What made this picture interesting was that their son, Daniel Shapiro, was in line to be the President of the New York United Jewish Appeal-Federation and was already a leader in the CJF.

I took very few days to settle in since I had but two years to do a great deal of work. I was delighted to get a phone call in our new apartment from Max Fisher, who was now the Chairman of the JAFI. Little did I know that I would get phone calls from Max at least five times each week? He simply wanted to be current on all activities. Irving Bernstein, the executive of UJA and Herbert Friedman's successor, told me that Max had the same calling pattern with him. I began working on staff development and struck out on my first two attempts with Cleveland and Chicago executives. But Carmi Schwartz, Executive Vice President, Metropolitan New Jersey Jewish Federation, took the gamble and became my Associate Director We worked with existing staff which included Charles Zibbell, Ted Comet, Frank Strauss and Nora Donegan. We were also able to attract three other young executives who gave us the kind of staff that I wanted. Robert Aronson, who later became the Detroit executive, Wayne Feinstein, the San Francisco executive, and Darrell Friedman, who got a great deal of personal advice and assistance from Marianne and me. He remained with Carmi and then went to Baltimore. This new staff, including Bruce Eisen, Financial Director, and existing staff gave us an excellent working organization.

There were three key elements to my two-year plan. The first was to develop a feeling by the local federations that we were available to come to their community and help. Each of our executive staff was made a consultant and assigned specific communities. I personally had four communities: New York, Miami, Los Angeles, and Chicago – and kept in contact with executives. For example, I went into Miami a number of times and helped them with specific problems.

A second element was to make sure that CJF's role with the Jewish Agency for Israel was different than it had been previously. I was not going to be the secretariat for the chairman. We would have a role but not anything like it had been. This would allow us to focus on our constituents community needs.

Third, we would focus on the communities' professional staffs' continuing education and training.

In addition, CJF had a major role in dealing with the immigration of Soviet Jewry. Our Washington office under Mark Talisman led the way.

In 1978, our office made sure the United States government imposed the demands of the Jackson-Vanik Amendment of the Soviet American Trade Bill on the Soviet Union, which was seeking most favored nation status. Because of United States demands, the Soviet Union under Brezhnev relaxed many of its inhumane restrictions and large numbers of Soviet Jews left, primarily for Israel.

I had personally done a study of JDC two years earlier in Italy, the outcome of which eased the movement from the Soviet Union through Italy to Israel.

By the end of 1978, a total of 250,000 Jews had left the Soviet Union, with about 160,000 going to Israel, and about 90,000 coming to the United States. The cost of re-settling them in the United States amounted to tens of millions of dollars, which was borne by the Jewish Feder-ations. Refugees, however, from other countries were re-settled with United State government aid. We, (CJF) and the Hebrew Immigrant Aid Society (HIAS), our working partner, brought this story of inequity to Congress and the administration. The U.S. government recognized its responsibility and through our office provided about fifty million dollars to match the sixty five million dollars the Jewish Federations had provided.

We also took leadership during the oil shortage in get-ting fuel to families in need. Once again, Mark Talisman took the lead on this.

The annual General Assembly (GA) and other quarterly meetings were in need of improvement. This was accom-plished by a committee that had been set up as a result of the study.

Morton L. Mandel was an outstanding President. We worked together on all the key issues and he gave per-sonal leadership to our federation constituency on many concerns, such as Jewish education.

I must describe my relationship with Irving Bernstein, executive head of UJA. As I earlier described, UJA was the agency created by JDC and UIA to raise funds for their respective services. We were extremely close and accepted each other's responsibilities. We consulted regularly and on my many trips to Israel during that period we always traveled together.

When we arrived in Israel, Chaim Venitzky would meet us and take us through the rigorous customs procedure. He was the JAFI's and UJA handler of all VIPs. Chaim always saw to it that our personal needs were met. He happened to be a very close personal friend of Baltimoreans, Jane and Marvin Shapiro. They had an apartment in Jerusalem and spent a good deal of time with Chaim and his wife, Nina. Jane was Zan Krieger's niece. She was a beautiful and charming lady who held a number of key leadership positions in Baltimore.

On a visit early in 1979, Chaim brought Irving and me a message from Prime Minister Menachem Begin, who asked to meet with both of us. After a series of factual inquiries he sat back and said he wanted each of our opinions on the question of Israel's greatest challenge in the coming decade. Irving indicated that he believed the extreme right wing posed the greatest threat. I indicated that religious fanaticism was Israel's greatest threat. Began was fascinated by our answers and thanked us profusely (unfortunately our answers proved to be correct).

I had let Max Fisher know that my role would be different than that of my predecessor with JAFI. However, at the start of my term on the board of JAFI (*ex-officio* because of my position) a number of JAFI board members were demanding that Max do something about changes in the operation that were needed. I worked with Max to create a process for board members to come together to work on the problems. We called it the Caesarea Process since the board spent a full week working on the problems in Caesarea. The Board of Governors learned from the process and actually developed a better level of functioning. Because of the outcome, I was able to move CJF out of its traditional role. Others such as UIA now took on more responsibility. This was a major change but I still had active participation in JAFI.

One specific delight I had in New York was being the guest of Morris W. Offit, my former Baltimore young leadership graduate. At the executive dining room of Salomon Bros, where he was a senior Vice President, he introduced me to his closest colleague, another senior Vice President, Michael Bloomberg. They told me that if one of them was not elevated to the presidency, which was in the offing, they were both going to leave. Salomon Brothers didn't, but they did.

The General Assembly (GA) of CJF was the largest and most representative assembly of North American Jewry. Every community was given a specific number of voting delegates based upon a logical formula. Others could be approved by their local federation to attend without vote. The GA usually lasted four days, culminating with a Saturday night dinner. Sunday morning was still a working day, but the Saturday night meeting could have had as many as 3,000 in attendance.

Morton L. Mandel and I worked with our planning committees and arranged for the first visit of an Israeli prime minister to a GA. At the 1980 GA in Detroit, Michigan, Prime Minister Menachem Begin and his wife were our guests and well over 3,000 delegates attended. Prime Minister Begin was a soft spoken, careful man of action, who laid out Israel's policy regarding the Soviet Union. He expressed Israel's tremendous appreciation for the role that the U.S. government was playing.

The preceding GA, held in Montreal, Canada in November of 1979, also had a very large attendance. The community delegates at that assembly were enthused because our study that had been delivered to them eight months earlier had suggested the ways in which communities could become deeply involved in CJF actions.

The four days of the GA provided time for a large number of meetings, seminars, and lecture presentations. Subjects covered every area of Jewish community life – education, culture, interrelations, agency activity, relationship to Israel, relations with U.S. government, fund raising, endowment development, etc. It entailed heroic work by our relatively small staff and our dedicated volunteers.

One specific study recommendation of the many on lay and professional personnel was to create a four-day annual training institute for professionals. When this was implemented it became a prize for professionals and was sought after competitively. Under the direction of my associate, Fern Katelman, these intense educational retreats were outstanding learning experiences. She brought in top-level teachers and practitioners to lead these sessions. In order to perpetuate the concept, I got my Baltimore friend, Louis Fox (past CJF President) to endow the project and to name it in honor of my predecessor, Philip Bernstein, who had served a dozen years as Executive Vice President.

My usual and apparently final push for a woman professional to lead a Big 16 Federation was to get Fern Katelman to apply for the next logical opening. She, however, opted to join Larry Moses as his assistant at the Wexner Foundation after I left CJF.

They were so many areas of involvement that could be recounted in my short twenty-four months at CJF, such as my seven visits to Israel and my frequent trips to Washington D.C. However, as my time was running out I kept getting urgent calls from Steven Solender, my Baltimore successor. He was pursuing me to return as the President of the Zanvyl Krieger Fund or he would not receive any funds from Mr. Krieger.

I reminded Steve that I was already two years behind in my personal plan, and that with my two years in New York coming to a conclusion, I was being pursued for private consultation. He finally convinced me to meet him and then see Mr. Krieger. I went to Baltimore in midsummer of 1980. Marianne joined me because we had planned to put our townhouse on the market and to begin living full time in Florida.

L-R: Robert Hiller, Marianne Hiller, Barbara Mandel, Morton Mandel. CJF President Mandel and Executive Hiller joined by wives at General Assembly of CJF, Detroit, MI. (Photo by Robert A. Cumins, Clifton, NJ)

UJA Executive, Irving Bernstein and JAFI Chairman, Max Fisher, confer at GA

**L-R: Marianne Hiller, Leah Rabin, Ambassador Yitzak Rabin, Bob Hiller.
Embassy Party, 1969**

L-R: Robert Hiller, **Morton** Mandel, and Prime Minister of Israel, Menachem Begin. CJF President Mandel and Ex VP Hiller Greet PM Begin at Detroit Airport and welcome him to CJF General Assembly, 1980.

L-R: Carmi Schwartz, Robert Hiller, Phillip Bernstein. Farewell gift presented to Robert I. Hiller on his retirement from CJF – 1981.

In our meeting with Steven Solender, he could barely contain himself. He knew that Zanvyl Krieger (Zan) was serious about his threat not to fund the Zanvyl and Isabelle Krieger Fund (ZK Fund) if I did not become its operating president. Steve knew it was his responsibility to make sure the ZK Fund became operative. I once again explained to him that I had already sacrificed two years and did not believe it was my responsibility for reselling Zan. Certainly someone else could lead the ZK Fund. I agreed, however, to talk with Mr. Krieger.

Zan was straightforward in our meeting. He said my relationship to him was more important to him then the ZK Fund. He explained that he felt like I was a family member, a brother, and he wanted someone like a brother in whom he had complete trust to lead the ZK Fund. He predicted many hundreds of millions of dollars would come to the ZK Fund and he believed I was the only person he knew that could creatively use and direct such a large amount of money. He asked, "why not do both – run the Fund and run your business?" He guaranteed that I would not lose any income because he would advise the ZK Fund that he was guaranteeing my compensation. I explained that if I were to do this I would determine when and where I would work. We came to an agreement and I was about to: 1) have my own consulting business and, 2) become the operating president of the ZK Fund.

The day my two-year CJF contract in New York was completed, Marianne and I planned to move back to Baltimore into our relatively new townhouse. Before this could happen, I agreed to have both of us present at a testimonial dinner. It was very moving and satisfying to get the heartfelt appreciation from the very top of the leadership of the American Jewish community.

We were back in Baltimore and Boca Raton. I planned on doing my consulting out of my Florida home and administering the ZK Fund from a very small office in the handsome new Associated Krieger Building.

My consulting business immediately became an overwhelming success. I could have worked full time with at least two assistants. I, however, limited the number of clients and the type of service that was required.

For example, I did comprehensive community studies of three west coast Jewish communities – Los Angeles, San Diego and Phoenix. The three studies took nearly two years. My work plan was to spend nine days a month, three days in each community. It worked well and the outcomes were very helpful to the three communities.

I included Baltimore nonprofits as clients, which I could do part time while I was working in the ZK Fund office. My clients were the best of Baltimore, including the Baltimore Symphony Orchestra, the Baltimore Museum of Art and the AJCWF.

A word about the Baltimore Symphony Orchestra (BSO): Bud Zamoiski (Bud) was the President at the time, John Gidwitz, the Executive Officer, and David Zinman, Conductor and Music Director. This was a successful and fun consult. Bud Z was probably among the two or three best solicitors I ever assisted. Gidwitz was the nephew of Joseph Gidwitz, Chicago, who was a principal in the search committee that I had turned down years before. David Zinman was brilliant and charming. In fact, I should have paid him to work with him. Bud Z was the quarterback and I was the coach. Several years later, I had the opportunity to entertain David Zinman and his wife in Aspen, Colorado, where we spent six weeks in the summer. He ultimately became head of the music school and festival in Aspen.

My largest client was the United Jewish Appeal and this required from two to three days per week at its office in New York City. Stanley Horowitz, the former Cleveland JCF executive had taken over from Irving Bernstein in 1983. Shortly after Stanley assumed that position, he called me for a consultation. The outcome was my assisting him as consultant. I would assist him in recruiting and training as well as a multitude of general problems.

I moved in and took over Alex Grass's (Chairman of the UJA Board) office, next to Stanley, and went to work. The first and immediate task was to recruit a campaign director. Morris Sherman was Campaign Director of the Los Angeles Jewish Federation. He had been a young Baltimore worker for whom I provided guidance and assistance all through his career. I convinced Morris to take the UJA position and he moved his family east.

I worked with Stanley and Morris in recruiting a full staff complement. Professional training was essential for this new staff. I designed and set up a training program for all of the new staff as well as some of the existing staff. Out of this group, several stars emerged. Yes, one star was a woman, Vicki Agron, who really grasped the total of our training. I've been told that she went on to be an executive in the merged CJF and UJA organization.

UJA had a sizeable field staff and a particularly good field operation in South Florida. This was headquartered in Deerfield Beach, just one community south of Boca Raton and fifteen minutes from my home. The Director of this operation was Jay Jacobson. I convinced Stanley to set up a recruitment and training center in this regional office. We engaged Carol Effrat, a top notch fund raising professional and teacher from Miami, to lead the recruitment and to do the training. It frequently happens that at least one of the trainees would be outstanding and have the skills and personality to move to the top of the profession. We found this star in Mark Terrill. He was the model graduate and today he is the acclaimed President of the Baltimore AJCWF.

One other unusual request for consultation came to me from two Jewish federations, both of which had sold their Jewish sponsored and owned hospitals. I first helped the top leadership of the Pittsburgh Jewish community deal with the net receipt of approximately one hundred million dollars. In a carefully designed sounding of the community, and working through the leadership of the community, a new Jewish community foundation was created.

Kansas City was the other Jewish community that sold its hospital for approximately a net of thirty-five million dollars. This consultation lasted about three months of intensive work, getting careful opinion from a broad cross section of the Jewish community. This required that I engage an assistant.

There were many professionals that had wanted to work with me in my new consulting business. I had, however, developed an idea and this gave me the opportunity to implement it. My oldest child, Karen Kriesberg, was a graduate of the School of Social Work, University of Maryland, and held an MSW, plus other advanced certifications. She was the Chief of Professional Services at the House of Ruth, the largest domestic violence agency in Maryland. Not only did she have a high level of professional skills, but she also was a great communicator. I offered her the opportunity to work with me if she could use her vacation time or get a leave of absence. She was excited by the idea and worked out the arrangements with her agency. She was so outstanding and engaging that the Kansas City leadership asked me if they could offer her the executive position in the study's proposed foundation. Karen and I had a great time working together on a most successful consulting job and we both agreed that she should not consider a new job offer at that time.

Another area of consulting was with existing or new foundations. The Saltzman Foundation, Cherry Hill, New Jersey, had a variety of problems which I helped them address through a consulting contract that put me on call to the executive and Board.

One of the most stimulating relationships I had was with the Wexner (Leslie) Foundation of Columbus, Ohio, and New York City. Rabbi Maurice Corson was the foundation president. My relationship with him started in Baltimore where he had been a new rabbi for one of the city's largest Conservative synagogues. He came from Philadelphia with an interesting background and credentials. He, however, seemed bored and uneasy with the routine of being a synagogue rabbi. When he and the congregation decided to part company, I assisted in getting him an executive position with the United Israel Appeal of Canada. He did so well that he was recruited to return to the U.S.A. in an executive position with International B'nai B'rith. Leslie Wexner met him through his work with B'nai B'rith, and when Les began to put together a formal foundation, he engaged Rabbi Corson as the chief executive.

I assisted Corson in the initial stages, and when he put together a distinguished advisory group, I agreed to serve as part of that advisory committee. The committee consisted of Dr. Robert Chazen, New York University Professor of Hebrew and Judaic Studies, Dr. Charles Leibman, Bar Ilan University, Political Scientist, Dr. John Ruskay, Vice President Jewish Theological Seminary (currently President of UJA Federation, New York City.)

This group met in Columbus, Ohio, and New York City and assisted Rabbi Corson in creating an unusual foundation with its own agenda and programming. I served for several years and then retired from this consulting role. Rabbi Corson and I continued our friendship and he re-

and he replaced me with Philip Bernstein, the former executive of CJF.

My consulting business attracted many unusual offers. For example, another consulting group proposed a merger with me being the chief operating officer. Another very successful consultant wanted me to do a joint venture with him. I, however, stuck to my original plan and limited my consulting intake.

I began to push Zan Krieger to put large funds into the ZK Fund, but he resisted. He felt that U.S. Surgical (USS) was growing and would be worth much more in a few years. My work with the ZK Fund was rather routine and at that time not professionally stimulating.

Zan's two daughters and I comprised the grant committee of the ZK Fund and we met at least quarterly. Betsy, the older daughter, consistently complained about her father and I could see how he would appear too self-interested. She had her own ideas and a value system that was approximately 180 degrees different from her father. I kept telling both daughters that they were going to be the stewards of a very large fund. I asked Betsy to stop complaining and do something positive. I kept pushing her to enroll in the University of Maryland School of Social Work, not necessarily to get a degree but to gain knowledge. She being very bright, not only enrolled, but got her MSW. She now was becoming an expert.

Jean, the younger sister, had an advanced degree in working with learning disabled children. I could see that when the ZK Fund was truly financed, and when Zan was no longer an outside influence, these two young women were going to create a fund that would lead the way in Baltimore and Maryland. That in my mind was my objective. It was coupled with the idea of finding my successor who could work with these two outstanding young women in leading the ZK Fund.

The first major grant that was made by the ZK Fund was one in which both Betsy and Jean had total disinterest. I explained to them that there would be many such grants and they had to keep close to the fund and learn. With my consistent prodding they did what had to be done.

The first major grant of the ZK Fund was in the field of Jewish Education. There were several Orthodox day schools in Baltimore, but none were Conservative or Progressive Judaism. Rabbi Joel Zaiman, Zan's Rabbi, and a friend of mine, was a visionary who documented the need for a nondenominational Jewish day school. It could be housed in his Chizuk Amuno synagogue's excellent educational facilities. He knew that using the Schechter School curriculum and guidelines (a national program under conservative auspices), he would be able to move ahead rapidly. I was sympathetic to his cause and Zan became very interested when we described it to him.

The Krieger Schechter Day School began in 1982 with just seventeen kindergarten and first graders. More than four hundred were enrolled within a decade, receiving a comprehensive academic program integrating Jewish and secular learning.

The ZK Fund initially gave the school a Five hundred Thousand Dollar challenge grant and over the succeeding years that total reached five million dollars.

Rabbi Zaiman, at a later date, became a board member of the ZK Fund, being nominated as a community trustee. He was a valuable and vocal edition. A few years later he wrote me a lengthy letter covering several subjects but with the following strong recommendations:

"... my thought is that you should consider writing your biography. There are so many books on Jewish interests being published now, some of the scholarly ones are really good. Most of the stuff on the Jewish community and how it works and what it means are garbage. You have more experience and know more about the American Jewish community than practically anyone. You have the advantage of a dual perspective – professional and lay. You understand the mentality of both and how they work. You have a storehouse of great stories. It would be a major lapse on your part ... to allow the field to the likes of ... et al. This is really a plea, Bob, to seriously consider writing your memoirs, but, friend, please do not take too long thinking about.. Do begin now ..."
" please think hard on this Bob. I'm not trying to compliment you at all ... that ain't my style."

Rabbi Joel Zaiman

It should be fairly obvious that I jumped at Rabbi Zaiman's prod and twenty-five years later, I took pen in hand. Some man of action! But the perspective is so much better twenty five years later.

Reading Rabbi Zaiman's letter, as I began to write this memoir, I recall that I have had unbelievable relations with the Rabbis. Many have been good friends and many close associates. I have written about several but there are several more that should be mentioned.

When I was seeking advice as to my life's work, one of the people that were very helpful was Rabbi Jerome Folkman, a Reformed Rabbi in Grand Rapids, Michigan, and a member of the city's school board. He was not my personal Rabbi, but a good friend who gave me excellent suggestions.

In Pittsburgh, after my associate Samuel Frankel chaired the UJF campaign, Rabbi Seymour Cohn, a Conservative Rabbi, came forward and led the 1958 campaign. He was an eloquent speaker and turned out to be a top-notch fundraiser. After I had praised him at several national meetings, he became the subject of a number of search committees. He ultimately left Pittsburgh and became the Rabbi of a large and well-known Chicago synagogue.

Life frequently has strange twists and turns of fate. In Pittsburgh, the Rabbi of a young and very successful suburban Mt. Lebanon congregation was Daniel Silver. He was the son of my dear friend, Abba Hillel Silver. Through mutual friends the Silver's, Dan and Adele, became social friends. They ultimately moved back to Cleveland where he succeeded his father.

One of the reasons I accepted the invitation to become the Executive Vice President of the AJCWF in Baltimore was the encouragement received from Rabbi Morris Lieberman, Baltimore Hebrew Congregation. He was a dynamic man of action. He was actively involved in the civil rights struggle and was an outspoken and involved friend of Israel. Because of him, I served for four years as a board member of the Baltimore Hebrew Congregation. We had many common interests and many mutual friends. My favorite story about Rabbi Lieberman had to do with his hearing aids. He had a slight hearing disability. Marianne and I would occasionally attend Friday evening services with Louis and Dorothy Fox. We would sit in the front row center. Rabbi Lieberman was an ardent Orioles baseball fan, just as we were. About every thirty minutes during services, he appeared to be adjusting his hearing aid, after which he would suddenly move his right hand with one finger and then his other hand with two. Morrie had the Orioles game plugged into his ear and he was giving Lou and me the score.

Rabbi Lieberman's assistant was Rabbi David Goldstein, a 6 foot 4 inch strapping young man. I was 6 foot 3 inches, and together about once a week, we made a formidable doubles tennis team. The normal size opponents who usually played with us had this vision of Moses holding the Ten Commandments, and Joshua waving a scripted social statement standing at the net confronting them. We were most intimidating.

On my frequent train trips between Baltimore and New York, I would occasionally meet Rabbi Jacob Agus, either going or returning from Philadelphia. He taught at Temple University, in addition to his rabbinical duties at a large Baltimore Conservative synagogue. We always had great discussions on the train since we differed on our attitude about Israel. He kept urging me to do him the favor of speaking on Sunday morning before his three hundred plus men's educational breakfast. I succumbed and we had an annual session for four or five years.

Rabbi Herman Neuberger, President of the Yeshivas Ner Yisroel, Baltimore's premier Orthodox institution, and I developed a long-standing friendship. He would give me advice on my dealings with the Orthodox community, and I, in turn, gave him frequent consultation on his dealing with secular issues. It was apparent that we were good friends, so I was not surprised that he made the benediction at the gala event honoring my service to Baltimore.

I had numerous social friends beyond my working colleagues. We vacationed with Carol and Samuel (Sandy) Frank. We attended the Baltimore Symphony Orchestra and the Baltimore Chamber Orchestra with Helen and Alfred Coplan, etc. etc. But my special friend, who took me fishing on his boat in the Chesapeake Bay, or with whom I flew to Costa Rica for sail fishing, was Bud Z. He even taught me bone fishing off Bimini.

Life was extremely full in Baltimore and I knew I had to reduce my private consulting workloads. This led me to intensify my push on Zan Krieger to move more of his funds into the ZK Fund.

Zanvyl Krieger was a many faceted human being. He, however, was predictable in many areas of his behavior. He had total trust in my judgment on most aspects of life. He trusted no one, however, but himself on business or investment decisions. Since he had planned well for his family, all of his remaining assets would ultimately go to the ZK Fund. In order for the ZK Fund to properly plan, it required some picture of when it would be funded. This led me to develop an actual strategy for getting him to move assets to the ZK Fund.

Zan loved to join me at lunch as often as I could schedule it. I developed and tried to have a regular Friday lunch with him at the Suburban Club. First, I had Bernard Manekin, then I added Leroy Hoffberger, then Louis Fox. The lunch guests were all members of the ZK Board. I then added Dr. Herman Goldberg and later Rabbi Zaiman when he became a board member. Zan was the only non-board member. I used to joke with the group about allowing Zan to meet with us since we gave him the honor of signing the check.

The Friday lunches were extremely valuable, because I used them to talk about issues and projects that were ZK

Fund related. It served as a testing and advisory session. I made sure the idea of funding was usually part of the discussion. We had significant funding to cover our immediate requirements, but I knew that we should have the ability to diversify the assets rather than all of them being in a single company.

At this time, Dr. Steven Mueller was President of Johns Hopkins University (JHU), and both Zan and I had been talking to him about an idea that would bring together several disciplines in an institute within the JHU. The purpose would be to study the mind and the brain. We speculated that it was possible that solutions and treatments may come from such studies. Dr. Mueller had several JHU department heads exploring this idea. One of the department heads was Dr. Guy McKahann, head of the medical school's Department of Neurology.

Guy was an exciting scientist and leader. He was also the key member of the new executive search committee of the Kennedy Institute, an independent organization that had affiliation with the JHU Medical School.

Since 1930, Kennedy Institute had been working to assist children with brain and trauma disorders. This had been Zan's one non-business continuous board activity. He had involved me in its work. Through that, I had met Dr. Guy McKahann, who was leading the search that ultimately brought Dr. Gary Goldstein to the Kennedy Institute as its new Director. So, not only was Guy playing a leading role in the recruitment of the executive of Kennedy Institute but he was the driving force in trying to get JHU to create the mind-brain institute.

This two-pronged story really unfolds with Dr. Goldstein's engagement and the beginning of a major capital fund campaign of the Kennedy Institute.

I was invited to lunch by Ronald E. Creamer, the Chairman of the Board of the Kennedy Institute, who asked for the ZK Fund's assistance in the campaign. I asked him if the Kennedy family was contributing. He indicated that they primarily lent their name and on occasion made a minimal contribution. I learned that the Board of Directors of Kennedy Institute had begun a three million dollar capital campaign. This was a compromise of the twenty five million dollars that really was required. I said that before I would discuss this with the Board of the ZK Fund, I wished to speak with Dr. Goldstein at length.

I met with Dr. Goldstein, and we spent a good deal of time going over the needs and possibilities of achieving a twenty five million dollar result. I explained to him that development was my business. But since Zan was a member of the Kennedy Board I would give Dr. Goldstein my evaluation and suggestions. We actually designed the plan.

The Board of Directors of Kennedy Institute had a good deal of potential for contributing funds. I met with Zan and briefed him on what I had been doing. I then had Zan meet with Dr. Goldstein and me. Before the meeting, I suggested to Zan that we propose making a challenge grant of five million dollars to the Kennedy Institute. The Kennedy Institute would raise two dollars for every dollar we contributed. Dr. Goldstein turned out to be a very good fund developer. He later was able to get the State of Maryland to match a good share of the challenge grant.

Long stories sometimes deserve short answers. I proposed all of this to the Board of the ZK Fund. They were very supportive and urged that we proceed. This was our largest contribution to date and the board felt that it could be a worthwhile beginning in support of children's services.

The Kennedy Institute Board was so thrilled with the support that we had given that they asked for a private meeting with me. Mr. Creamer, Chairman, asked me if I knew of some way that Kennedy Institute could honor Zan. Could they name a building? Could they create a special program? I told him that I had a suggestion and they could either accept or reject it. I said that the Kennedy name was worthwhile on the institution but that the Krieger name was what could give life to the institution. I suggested that the Krieger name be added. My proposal was that it be called the Kennedy Krieger Institute.

Because the Kennedy Krieger Institute was doing such important work, the ZK Fund contributed more than six million dollars additional in the next few years. The Kennedy Krieger Institute today, as was at that time, considered by many authorities as the premier medical and research center for children with traumatic disabilities.

I always thanked Guy McKahann for being a party to bringing Gary Goldstein to Baltimore, but Guy was to play another enormous role in the JHU and ZK Fund relationship. I, on the other hand, agreed to serve on the

Board of Kennedy Krieger Institute, the only agency I would serve in that capacity.

The Board of JHU did not give Dr. Mueller much encouragement for the development of a mind brain institute because of costs and because it was a totally new departure from JHU's traditional way of doing scientific investigation and teaching.

Guy McKahann was undaunted in his quest for JHU to become a leader in this endeavor. He continued actively to pursue this with President Mueller and with me.

I finally brought Zan Krieger into the discussion because the concept intrigued me and because Guy agreed to lead the new institute if it could be funded. I needed Zan to contribute at least ten million dollars to the ZK Fund, which he ultimately did.

Dr. McKahann finally had his wish. In 1987, he got JHU approval and a grant of eight million dollars from the ZK Fund. As he explained it, we could now explore how the brain worked and how disease and injury changed its functioning. The scientists in the Institute now examined how the whole mind functions and how it processes information.

The ZK Fund subsequently granted another four million dollars to the Krieger Mind Brain Institute. *A personal note*: Since I had such high hopes for the Institute, I arranged for my grandson to volunteer and spend a summer working with the scientists. My daughter Barbara's son, Zev, was so greatly influenced by his experience that it was one of the contributing factors to his becoming a psychiatrist. He was Board Certified last year and has become a specialist in addiction.

I kept thanking Zan for contributing large funds for such challenging new projects. He in turn lavished praise upon me for having given him the opportunity to do innovative and worthwhile undertakings. We met frequently and I always kidded him by saying "with your money and my chutzpah we can do anything." In fact, our work did bring us together to the extent that I became his advisor on most of his activities. With the passing of Milton Schiller, I urged him to bring in new legal counsel from his firm. Howard Miller had been doing his tax work and did a major part of the legal work when Zan bought the Lord Baltimore Hotel. Howard shortly became a public appointed member of the ZK Fund Board.

Howard Miller is a down to earth, plain talking attorney. We developed an exceptional relationship - just one example describes how we worked. Both Howard and I looked after Zan's children from a fiscal and financial standpoint. Zan had properly cared for his grandchildren's economic future several years previously. There was, however, a new granddaughter and both Howard and I developed a plan for her to receive similar benefits as the other grandchildren. We explained this to Zan and it was implemented. I also stepped aside as a board member of the Kennedy Krieger Institute after Howard had been elected to that Board. He had moved up into a leadership position on that board. I was loading Howard up with work from the ZK Fund. He never protested my actions and I never apologized for them. I knew that at some point he would play an important role on the ZK Fund Board. But even with Howard's help, I still had resistance from Zan on transferring one half or more of his USS stock to the ZK Fund. He knew that we would want to create a more business-like portfolio. He felt, however, that he was doing the right thing.

Zan's nephew, Dr. Herman Krieger Goldberg, a noted ophthalmologist, was a family member of the ZK Fund Board. He kept educating me on a number of medical fronts. He was on both the Johns Hopkins University Hospital staff and the Sinai Hospital staff. He took me to a variety of medical meetings, which included such subjects as alternative medicine. A former Baltimore City championship tennis player, he was my tennis "coach," and frequently invited me to play in his much higher level tennis games. Most important he gave me insight into medical education practice and politics.

Dr. Guy McKahnn, Chief Executive, Krieger Mind Brain Institute, JHU

Dr. Gary Goldstein, President, Kennedy Krieger Institute.

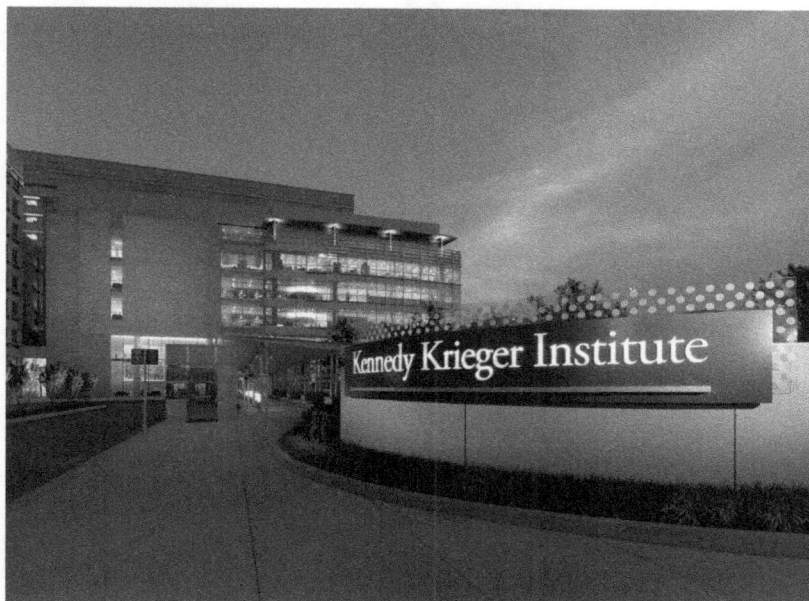

Entrance to Kennedy Krieger Institute

The Wilmer Eye Institute at Johns Hopkins Hospital was under the leadership of Dr. Arnall Patz from 1979 through 1989. Not only was Wilmer Eye Institute considered to be the ultimate in eye care and research, but Patz was recognized as probably the leading ophthalmologist of this time. He was the recipient of the Presidential Medal Of Freedom and he also received the Albert Lasker Award (America's Nobel Prize) for his work on the causes and prevention of blindness. Arnall was the son-in-law of Lester Levy, who was a key member of the search committee that had brought me to Baltimore. Eleanor, Mrs. Lester Levy, and her daughter Ellen, Arnall's wife, were outstanding women in their own right. Marianne and I were very good friends of both couples. I felt very close to Arnall, which brought me into close proximity to the Wilmer Eye Institute.

With Dr. Herman Goldberg on one side of me and Dr. Patz on the other side, it stands to reason that I would have developed an unusual interest in ophthalmology and in Wilmer Eye Institute and Sinai Hospital's Department of Ophthalmology. I wanted to do something major and on the cutting edge in this field. Zan loved the idea when I explored it with him and he actually ended up pushing me.

Six years after my return to Baltimore, I was involved in a consultation in Israel. I was working on different aspects of its healthcare and hospital system. This led me to the Office of the Surgeon General of the Israel Defense Forces, Dr. Yehuda Danon. He was responsible for not only health care for the military, but also led the way for Israel to aid other countries in times of medical emergencies, such as earthquakes and floods.

After my interview on the study, Dr. Danon and I had lunch and an immediate affinity developed between us. He told me about a new children's hospital that was being created in Peta Tikvah, a town just north and east of Tel Aviv. He told me that the hospital would become a bridge to peace because it would be open to children of all neighboring countries, as well as all the children of Israel. He was going to be the director of the new hospital. We talked about ophthalmology which is a critical part of children's medical services. I promised to return and visit the hospital, which was slated to open in about two years, in 1991. This was a promise I wanted to keep.

I began to develop a strategic plan for the field of ophthalmology. The plan was simple, the implementation was complex, and "crazy impossible" as described by one of my board members. I pointed out to my board that sometimes opportunities have to be made.

My plan was to start with Sinai Hospital and to upgrade the Department of Ophthalmology. It would be an institute with a direct relationship to the hospital's chief executive. When this part of the plan was implemented, the Sinai Krieger Eye Institute was created. It was not only a service and research center, but a teaching center. The ZK Fund Board was thrilled with this development and made a multi-million dollar commitment. In my mind, there was a huge missing link in what we had developed.

The Krieger Eye Institute had to have a full affiliation with Wilmer if it was going to attract top-level personnel and if it was to be a great teaching center. Members of the Board of the ZK Fund again said that I was simply chasing a dream, but I wanted and received the Board's backing to make the dream come true.

My relationship with Dr. Patz was helpful, but so was an intermediate step that I planned. I took Zan with me to see the Pediatric Eye Center at Wilmer. I had seen it, but when Zan saw the Center, crowded into a basement, he was appalled. Now he pushed me. It also motivated him to contribute more of his USS stock to the ZK Fund.

Dr. David Guyton, a renowned pediatric ophthalmologist, led the department that was doing unusual work despite its inadequate facilities. After consulting with Dr. Guyton and Wilmer Chief, Dr. Patz, the ZK Fund presented Wilmer Eye Institute with a One-and-a-Quarter-Million-Dollar challenge grant. It was quickly matched by two million five hundred thousand dollars and immediate action was untaken to create the new facility.

Now that the ZK Fund had made a major gift to Wilmer Eye Institute, I pursued Dr. Patz with my proposal. The main issue was an agreement for a joint relationship between Wilmer Eye Institute and the Sinai Krieger Eye Institute, with Wilmer being given the opportunity to nominate the chief of staff of Sinai Krieger Eye Institute. Interns and residents would rotate through both. The costs of operating the joint relationship would be covered by Sinai Krieger Eye Institute. The ZK Fund would annually contribute a specific amount to Sinai Krieger Eye Institute to cover the cost as long as the relationship would be in force. There were a number of other conditions that were worked out.

Dr. Irvin P, Pollack, practitioner and teacher on both staffs, was nominated by Wilmer as the new Chief and approved by Sinai Krieger Eye Institute. The affiliation was confirmed by both institutions and the ZK Fund approved the financing. This joint endeavor had one more piece in my plan, not primary, but unusual and valuable.

Marianne joined me on a visit to Israel, which we took with the Israel Tennis Centers, which really is a children's program, and it was so named a few years later. I wanted to see the program first hand and present the ZK Fund with a grant proposal. Ira and Gloria Boris were volunteer leaders of the Israel Tennis Centers who accompanied us on this trip. After completing my work with the Israel Tennis Centers, Marianne and I spent the next two days under the auspice of Dr. Yehuda Danon at the Israel Children's Hospital (later named Schneider Children's Hospital). Visiting the children's hospital, I felt like we were in an Arab country. Nearly all of the patients and their families appeared to be Arabs. We learned that approximately forty percent of the patients were Arab. All patients received the same professional services and loving care. It was truly a sight and epitomized the "bridge to peace." I worked out a multi-faceted program, which included an endowment for the chairmanship of the Department of Ophthalmology and an initial grant to establish the Krieger Community Services for Pediatric Ophthalmology. This service brought eye care to a network of eleven clinics throughout Israel.

Another important part of our contribution was a one-and-a-quarter-million-dollar educational endowment to train Israeli doctors in pediatric ophthalmology at the Sinai Krieger Eye Institute and the Wilmer Eye Institute. There was no such training in Israel. It would be a one or two year training for doctors in eye care who would serve when they returned to Israel in the community clinics.

Finally, we created a five-hundred-thousand-dollar bridge to peace endowment to support a biannual conference for Israel and neighboring countries' ophthalmologists to advance their specialized training.

Our work brought the Israel Children's Hospital into an educational and training relationship with Baltimore's two great ophthalmological centers Wilmer Eye Institute and Sinai Krieger Eye Institute.

We now had delivered the total planned ophthalmology program that we had envisioned. This was an unusual undertaking. We created the opportunity and we made and implemented the decision.

The accomplishment of the ZK Fund and the regular Friday luncheon discussions with the key public board members began having a real impact on Zan Krieger. Jeffrey Waranch, with whom I spoke daily, was Zan's long time broker, as well as my personal broker. He told me that Zan had given him permission to advise me that he was planning to move a large number of USS shares to the ZK Fund. Two important changes were in motion.

Zan was relieved of his active duties on the Board of USS, and was now in an emeritus role. I also was discussing with him the idea of engaging investment counsel for the ZK Fund. This was accomplished, but too late. In September 1993, USS stock fell from its high of $134.50 per share to $22.50 a share. Fortunately, Zan had contributed about one hundred million dollars' worth of the stock to the ZK Fund prior to the drop. He had been motivated to do this because of a public health project I was developing, and in which he became interested. I had been briefing him on this project and he was very enthusiastic about it.

I had other projects, not as grand in mind, but in the works. I was now practically giving up my consulting business and devoting all of my working time to the ZK Fund.

L-R: Dr. Irvin and Marlene Pollock, Dr. Peter and Jan McDonnell, Ellen and Dr. Arnall Patz (deceased).

World renowned Ophthalmologist, Dr. Arnall Patz, former chair and head of Wilmer, JHU, and wife Ellen, meet with current Wilmer Chief, Dr. Peter McDonnell and wife Jan and Dr. Irvin Pollock, original and longtime Chief of Sinai Krieger Institute, and wife Marlene.

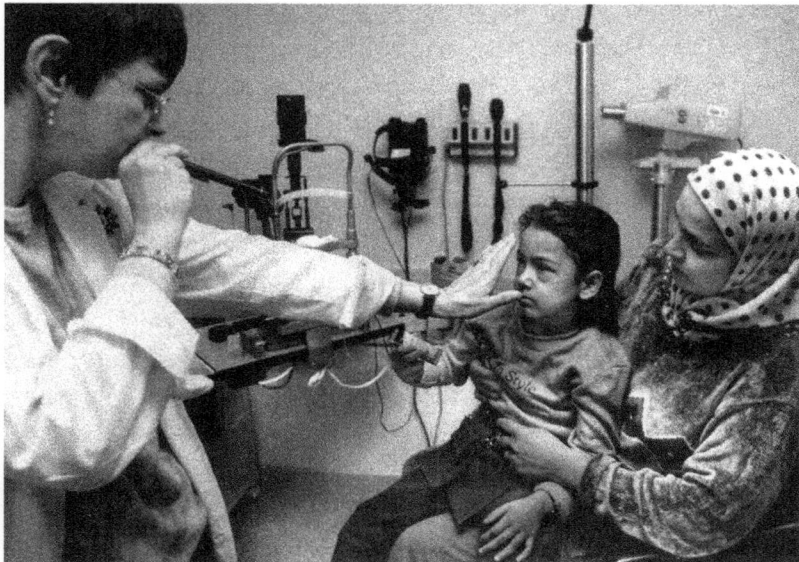

Children's Medical Center, Israel – eye to eye for Palestinian child

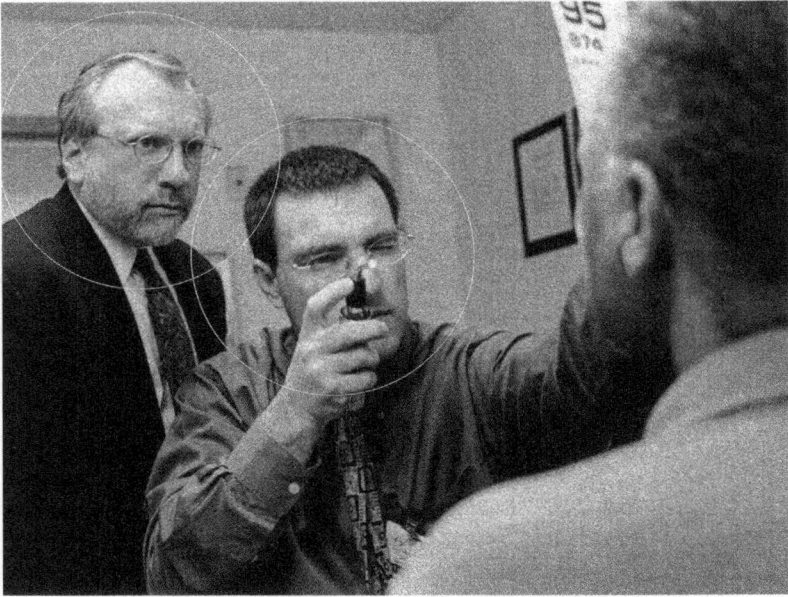

Israeli physician being trained at Sinai Krieger Eye Institute

Baltimore Mayor Kurt Schmoke joins Dr. Irvin Pollock, Zan Krieger and Robert Hiller at dedication of Sinai Krieger Eye Institute.

Zan and I had a close relationship with Robert (Bob) Weinberg. Zan from his law firm and I from Bob's active work on behalf of the AJCWF. Bob was an officer of the Jewish Historical Society of Maryland, an affiliated organization of AJCWF. He had a dream of creating a Jewish heritage center – museum, library and cultural center. He estimated the cost to be about one million dollars, but equally important was an endowment for a part time curator costing probably about twenty-thousand dollars a year.

Bob got Baltimore Mayor, William Donald Schaefer, to back the concept if Bob could show Baltimore Jewish community support. The Mayor's support was crucial because of zoning, parking and redevelopment issues.

Bob Weinberg met with me to see if I could bring the idea before the ZK Fund. I urged him to meet with Zan, which he did. I presented the idea to the ZK Board and got its full support with a minimal grant. It was the Board support that gave the concept credibility. Bob and the members of the Jewish Historical Society were able to raise approximately two million dollars to do the whole job.

The outcome of this activity was the Jewish Museum of Maryland. Bob passed away far too soon to see what an inspiring institution he had fathered.

One of my early activities when I was the Executive Vice President of AJCWF, was to urge and give support to the Baltimore Community Foundation (BCF). I always had in mind to develop one of the ZK Fund's interests that could be undertaken by the Baltimore Community Foundation. Tim Armbuster, President of Baltimore Community Foundation, and I had worked on a number of community projects, so I felt comfortable sharing my idea with Tim. I told him I wanted to get the Board of the ZK Fund to invest in a program that would help meet the needs of inner city children. Not just to provide services but to get community leaders – policy makers and professionals – to understand what was needed. Tim was excited about the project and we went to work.

The ZK Fund Board enthusiastically approved a half million-dollar grant to BCF to create an endowment. This led to a series of programs which were quickly put into place – accurate collecting of data on children in Maryland, educating community leaders about at risk children and the need for the immunization of children entering kindergarten. The ZK Fund contribution attracted an additional three million dollars to expand and continue this work.

Baltimore was proud of its Inner Harbor development for many reasons, but primarily as a tourist attraction. Rebecca Hoffberger, the wife of Leroy, ZK Board member, was a creative energetic and brilliant woman. After much effort she finally got me to accompany her to the foot of Federal Hill from which I could see practically the total Inner Harbor. While I enjoyed the view, Rebecca gave me a lecture of more than two hours, which had me totally absorbed. I first learned about "visionary art" which I had known as outsider art. This was work done by untrained artists, generally with some outside inspiration or vision. Frequently such work was found in institutions where disturbed persons used it as a means of expression. Such work was becoming more and more valuable. Some of the artists were already well known. Rebecca was a student of "visionary art."

She foresaw a museum that was designed to properly display such art. As we stood at the foot of Federal Hill, she pointed out to me three long warehouses on my right, as I stood facing the Inner Harbor. She said that the city was prepared to give her the warehouses for a museum if she could implement her vision. She had already taken three important additional steps. First, she had an architect work with her on a sketch to demonstrate what and how a museum would look. Second, she got our Senator, Barbara Mikulski, to have a congressional resolution passed making the proposed museum the official "Visionary Art Museum" of the United States of America. This had a number of benefits, including access to all federally funded facilities, and their artworks. Finally, she had gotten some foundation funding – not enough to start, but enough to cover her preliminary expenses. She wanted the ZK Fund to make a major contribution. I explained to her that this would be a very difficult sell, and would require a good deal of education of the ZK Board. I agreed to work through some of the issues, and to advise her how and whether I could proceed.

I tested the idea with my Friday lunch group of ZK Fund Board members. Leroy, Rebecca's husband, was part of this group, and he jumped in enthusiastically with a good discussion on a description of "visionary art."He demonstrated how the proposed museum could become a leading attraction, but most important he indicated that the Hoffberger Foundation would be making a sizeable grant. I observed Zan carefully during the discussion and concluded that he might be supportive of a reasonable proposal because of his affection for Leroy and Rebecca.

I took Zan on a visit to Federal Hill. He quickly saw the real estate benefit of the location, and of the city of Baltimore's offer of the warehouses.

After further consultation with Rebecca, I presented a suggested proposal to the ZK Fund Board. I described the proposed museum, with about forty thousand square feet of new exhibition space plus exhibition space in one of the converted warehouses, and a sculpture garden. My suggestion was that we make a grant of two million dollars. The Board finally accepted the suggestion, and the American Visionary Art Museum (AVAM) had its first major gift. This helped launch the museum's fund raising. Because of the creditability it gained from our grant, the AVAM was an architectural delight. It won the Urban Land Institute National Award for Excellence. It was to become an enormous success from the standpoint of visitor attendance. This was truly cutting edge risk taking, a major reason for foundation existence. Our support of

AVAM, the Jewish Museum of Maryland, and the Balti-more Community Foundation all demonstrated the ZK Fund's support for the City of Baltimore.

The panoramic view that Zan Krieger and Robert Hiller viewed from the foot of Federal Hill.

Rebecca Hoffberger, founder and director of AVAM with matchstick sculputure of her created by Gerald Hawk, famous visionary artist who was the first person to "walk through the doors on opening day" (American Visionary Art Museum, Baltimore, MD.)

While working in Pittsburgh, I developed a keen appreciation for the field of public health. Dean Cecil Shepps, of the University of Pittsburgh School of Public Health and I had worked and taught together. I had learned a great deal from him and he often claimed that my approach to community work was helpful in advancing his work in public health. When I came to Baltimore, the home of Johns Hopkins University (JHU), which included the largest graduate school of public health, I became acquainted with the school and its dean. Dean Dr. Alfred Sommer was an absolute delight. He not only was a charming and attractive man, but was brilliant and an outstanding academic. We quickly became close friends and he made sure that I saw every part of the school. He also insisted that I become fully acquainted with not only his curriculum, but also the student body. I took my friend Zan Krieger on several visits to the school so that we had common ground for discussions. I actually forced Zan to join me in attending one of the hearings that was conducted on the proposed health bill coming before Congress. I had to promise him that Hillary Clinton was not going to be a participant.

I began a carefully designed agenda to have the ZK Fund become the lead and main contributor for a totally new facility, which was desperately needed. Dr. Sommer and I worked together in estimating the need and costs. My estimate was approximately thirty million dollars.

I began talking with some of the ZK Fund Board members and even shared some of my thoughts with Zan Krieger. He was interested enough that he contributed a thirty million dollar gift to the ZK Fund in USS stock. He did this several months before the stock had a disastrous fall.

It was getting cold in Baltimore, so Marianne and I opened our Boca Raton house, and I worked from there. I planned on staying in Florida for a month before returning to Baltimore for meetings.

One beautiful sunny winter morning with the temperature around 70 degrees, I was working at my desk when I received a call from Dr. William Richardson (Bill), President of Johns Hopkins University. We knew each other well from our numerous joint activities. I kidded him about the cold weather in Baltimore and he responded that he wanted to come to Florida to visit me. I opened my calendar and asked him when he was planning on being in Florida. No, he wanted to come tomorrow to talk to me. A bit stunned, I suggested I could come back to Baltimore earlier than I planned if it was urgent. "How about a couple of weeks from now?" He wanted to see me tomorrow. "Okay, what time?" He told me he already had the tickets and that he and Rip Haley, Vice President of Development, would be at my home at 1:00 p.m. if that was okay. He would tell me about the purpose of the visit when we would be together tomorrow.

Of course, for the next twenty-four hours, I was doing mental gymnastics. Dr. Richardson was a no nonsense strong leader. In the short time he had been in Baltimore, he had gained the respect of all who had worked with him. He was not only an educator, but an executive that I admired. I surmised he wanted to discuss the possible ZK Fund contributions to the School Of Public Health. But why the rush?

After Marianne served coffee and our brief hellos, Bill Richardson gave me a full briefing on the purpose of his visit. It was clear and concise and he gave me all the time I needed for information and clarification.

I remember the story in detail because it placed a unique opportunity and a critical decision in my lap; certainly one of the most important decisions of my career.

My summary of our discussion began with Bill reminding me that JHU began in 1876, and was the first research university in the United States. He recalled the great growth and achievements of JHU, particularly the world recognition of the medical school and hospital and the academic acclaim of the School of Engineering. He reminded me that JHU was not only the largest employer in Baltimore, but in the State of Maryland. In essence, it was among the top universities of the world but also a bulwark of the State of Maryland's economy.

JHU had very successful fund raising and development of its medical enterprise – the School Of Medicine and Hospital. Individuals and corporations were supportive of those endeavors, but the School of Arts and Science was being starved to death.

Dr. Richardson made the point that "without the base of arts and sciences, the total university could not flourish, but would be diminished." He had spelled this out for his own Board and they were looking to him to solve the problem, to save the university. His predecessors had not been able to successfully deal with the problem, and so, at this point, it was now critical.

In answer to my questions, he indicated that what was required was a massive endowment infusion that would produce sufficient income to attract top academics, and would give budgetary stability to the School of Arts and Sciences. This in turn would give strength to the total university. I quickly got the impression that if this was not accomplished, both short and long term crisis would undermine the future development of JHU.

I simply asked him if failure to achieve this huge endowment would seriously affect the University and the State of Maryland. He concurred. "But how much is the minimum requirement?" I questioned. Both he and Rip Haley told me an absolute minimum of one hundred million dollars, probably one hundred twenty-five million dollars was the minimum requirement. I concluded that it was all or nothing. Without the total, a lesser or small amount would prolong the agony.

What did Dr. Richardson want from me? He had done his homework well. He started by telling me that he had discussed this with Dr. Sommer, who had agreed that the future of the University took precedence, even over the School of Public Health. President Richardson had concurred that the School of Public Health plan would be put aside if it in any way affected the endowment requirement of the School of Arts and Sciences.

Dr. Richardson quickly ticked off what the ZK Fund had already done for JHU – ten million dollars Mind and Brain Institute; two million dollars Wilmer; plus other smaller gifts totaling approximately fifteen million dollars. He said that what was needed was a sixty-five million contribution. Now I understood why he flew to Florida to see me. The University had never received a gift of even fifty million dollars for endowment. Dr. Richardson reminded me that Zan was a graduate of the School of Arts and Sciences and that it would be a logical connection.

Our conversation continued with a number of questions from me about how the endowment would be used, how and by whom the additional sixty million dollars would be raised, and how quickly he would require a response from me.

He reminded me that my friend, Morris W. Offit, was Chairman of the Board, and that Michael Bloomberg was the fund raising chairman. His final response was he would like to know "as soon as possible." I thanked Bill and Rip for flying to see me. I told them that after I recuperate from the immense burden they had asked me to share, I would get to work. I promised nothing but an exploration.

Before I packed my bag, I called my office with information I wanted from AJCWF's Financial Director, from Jeffrey Warench, my broker confidant, and from the consultant to AJCWF's investment committee. When I walked into my office, the information was on my desk. From that information, I concluded that thirty million dollars invested in primarily growth stocks, but with some other investments, and compounded annually, we could provide about fifty three million dollars in four plus years. This was crucial to my meeting with the ZK Fund Board, though this estimate was for me, and only for the Board, when it would be approved.

I met with Zan and shared with him the call and the business I had with President Richardson and Vice President Haley of Johns Hopkins University, both whom he knew well. I explained to him that I needed a few days to develop a plan, but first I needed to know his feelings about what was put into my lap. He was exhilarated by the opportunity, but he was dumbfounded by the position in which JHU found itself.

He absolutely wanted to help if we could afford it. I suggested that he come to the ZK Fund Board meeting, but let the Board members do the talking. He and I would make whatever refinements were needed if the Board wanted to move ahead. We both knew the Board would want to accept the challenge, if we could afford it. I did not at this time share with Zan my investment and funding analysis.

The Board accepted my plan with several good suggestions. The plan was simple. The ZK Fund would give JHU a challenge grant of up to fifty million dollars, to be matched by JHU two dollars for every one dollar, up to a total of one hundred million dollars raised by JHU. It had to be raised in no more than five years. If the grant was matched, the ZK Fund would have the right to designate certain specific parts of the endowment for naming purposes. I was to be given authority to work out the financing with the approval of the Board. This was the largest endowment gift JHU had ever received. Because the donor of our funds was a graduate of the school being endowed, which made it possible for us to make the grant, I suggested that the school be named after our donor, Zanvyl Krieger.

I met privately with Dr. Richardson to share with him the ZK Fund Board response and to give him the opportunity to discuss, and if necessary, to modify any of the conditions. He was most appreciative of what we had done and indicated he would get the authority to proceed.

We proceeded with some specific naming of the endowment and the formal necessary legal documentation of approvals. We had accepted the JHU challenge and JHU accepted our challenge for the benefit of JHU, and the people, and the community that it served.

I asked Morris W. Offit, Chairman of the Board of JHU, to meet with me and I presented my financing plan to him. I explained that we could invest the thirty million dollars that the ZK Fund had reserved, and based upon my estimates, which I shared with him, in five years it should exceed the fifty million dollar commitment. My preference, however, was to give the thirty million dollars to JHU and to have JHU invest it as a separate fund for five years. If my estimates were wrong, JHU could come back to the ZK Fund. If my estimates were correct, the extra, approximately three million-plus dollars would be designated by the ZK Fund for JHU endeavors. Morris liked the idea of JHU getting the funds immediately. He arranged for the special fund to be set up and to have a committee consisting of Michael Bloomberg, Chairman of JHU campaign, Morris W. Offit, Chairman of the Board of JHU, and Robert I. Hiller, President of the ZK Fund to receive quarterly reports from their investment advisor.

The invested fund ended up with the predicted fifty three million plus dollars in four years. The ZK Fund was therefore able to contribute about one-half of the three million dollar overage to the School of Public Health, which was used for a joint program with the Krieger School of Arts and Sciences.

I met with and congratulated Dr. Richardson for his grasp of the problem, and for his required aggressive approach to its solution. I thanked Morris for his usual calm and businesslike understanding of my financial plan and for his unusual leadership of JHU. Finally, I congratulated Zan for his making the funds available and his allowing me to work with the ZK Fund on this historic achievement. My trusted paradigm was in fact confirmed. I had been in the right place at the right time with the right credentials, but also with the right financial backing.

Just before we had completed our work on the Krieger School of Arts and Sciences, one of my ZK Fund Board members, and a very special friend of mine, died. Louis J. Fox was on the search committee that brought me to Baltimore. He was my first board President, though I had to relinquish him to CJF shortly after I arrived. He worked closely with me on the "Letter of Intent" program and he was my partner in getting Zan to endow the Associated Krieger Building. Louis and I had lunch together about every two weeks in addition to our informal weekly ZK Fund luncheons at the Suburban Club. In 1994, his health began to fail. I could not abandon my good friend, who was ten years my senior, so I made sure we were together for lunch every ten days or so. The last few months I actually carried him into the restaurant but he wouldn't miss the opportunity. During his last months, I shared with him my plans for the ZK Fund endowing the School of Public Health. The last week in February of 1995 he passed away. His family asked me to present the memorial talk at his funeral. Since he was a past President of the Baltimore Hebrew Congregation, the funeral was held at the Temple. It was filled to overflowing. After the Rabbi eulogized Louis, I spoke for ten minutes. The family and his friends told me it was the best speech of my life. I had lost a good friend and good friends are "hard to come by."

Four years later, 1999, I had triple bypass heart surgery at Johns Hopkins Hospital. Marianne and I decided to begin my retirement. My colleague and friend, Zan, was now unable to walk and was confined to a wheelchair. With the exception of one month following my surgery, we never missed seeing each other a couple of times each week. We shared not only his financial situation, but all of his ideas and personal thoughts with me.

Less than a month after my surgery, I arranged a meeting with Howard Miller and Zan at his apartment. I presented them with my plan for retirement, which would begin in about nine months. Zan was in tears, but very cogent. He told me that he wanted to leave me a major bequest and asked Howard to arrange this. I thanked him but, in fact, declined any gift or bequest. I explained that though we were dear friends and close associates, I was the professional head of a foundation and received compensation for my employment. I told Howard not to change Zan's will because if there were a bequest, it would be contributed to the ZK Fund.

The purpose of the meeting was not about me, but rather about the ZK Fund. I told Zan that I was recommending to AJCWF that Howard should succeed me as President, but not as the chief operating officer of the ZK Fund. That role should have a professional and I recommended Karen Kriesberg, my daughter, who had been engaged a year earlier as our Program Director. I explained to Zan that AJCWF would certainly appoint Karen, but if he wished, he could make it his suggestion. Zan's daughters, Betsy and Jean, insisted on Karen's appointment since she was their only choice. Howard agreed with the proposal and expressed his humble appreciation for the confidence that both Zan and I had in him.

I told Zan that there was one more major gift that I was going to propose to the ZK Fund and I wanted him to know about it. The Associated Krieger Building was the center of not only Jewish organizational life, but it had become the center for a great deal of the nonprofit organizational life of the total community. The building was ten years old. Fortunately, when we had planned it we had it structurally built to take an expansion. I asked Howard to make sure that a major contribution (more than one million dollars) would be granted by the ZK Fund for the expansion. The expansion did take place a number of months later.

I also explained to Zan that I wanted to make sure that after both of us were gone, the total assets of the ZK Fund would be at least between forty and fifty million dollars. From the annual income, I wanted to also confirm that the annual gift to the AJCWF would not go below its present level.

The transition to Howard and Karen was approved and geared to be fully implemented by the spring of 1999. In the meantime, instead of my carrying Zan as I had Louis Fox, I pushed him in his wheelchair as we visited some of our old haunts.

Once again my master schedule was a bit off. I was twenty years late in retirement, but then I did run a business and operate a major foundation in those twenty years.

I was back home in Florida at the end of August. I received a call from Betsy Krieger and Karen asking if I could come back to Baltimore since Zan was not doing well. I spent as much time as possible with him the next several weeks.

Zan enjoyed my recalling some of the good times we had together. I reminded him of how the only time I could see him back in the 70's was when I would meet him at the ballpark. I would sit between Milton Eisenhower, President of JHU, his buddy and Zan. While I talked business, they debated baseball coaching strategy. I chided Zan about his holding on to USS stock. I even took him in his wheelchair to the Kennedy Krieger Institute's new High School, for which the ZK Fund has made a significant contribution.

In the middle of September, Zan passed away.

Rabbi Zaiman made an eloquent eulogy. I looked out over the packed Chizuk Amuno Synagogue. I saw people from nearly every organization to whom the ZK Fund has contributed; baseball and football leaders and players; government officials; and a large number of Krieger Schechter schoolchildren and their families. I took a minute or two longer than usual in my eulogy. Everyone in that synagogue knew that Zan's memory would live on because we had created a Fund that would be doing good things for Baltimore, for Maryland, the Jewish community, and for the institutions that make a community a better place in which to live. I told the assembly in closing, that we should have solace and joy because few people have their dreams come true. Today we were bidding *adieu* to a man who actually saw that happen.

Two days after the funeral, Marianne and I flew home to Florida.

Associated Krieger Building with new addition.

At home in Florida with the Hillers. L-R:
1st row: Marianne and Bob
2nd Row: Barbara, Josh, Karen

Howard Miller, new Chairman of ZK Fund
Board and Karen Kreisberg, New Executive
Director

L-R: - first row, R. Hiller, Howard Miller, 2nd row: Betsy Krieger, Jean Kahn. Betsy and Jean with retiring president Hiller and Howard Miller, New Chairman of ZK Fund

EPILOGUE

I had asked my son, Josh, and daughter in-law, Cindy, to review the draft of my book. When they called me with several suggestions, Josh asked me an interesting question. He said I had placed great importance on the formal training programs I had developed for volunteer and professional leadership. I had not, however, described leaders who epitomized the objective of this training. He questioned whether "such stars ever emerged." When I answered the question, it was clear that from both volunteer and professional training "stars emerged."

The volunteer programs, identified as young leadership training programs, had several outstanding graduates. But it is interesting to note that graduates of my last class in both Cleveland and Baltimore achieved the ultimate level of leadership: Morton L. Mandel from Cleveland and Morris W. Offit from Baltimore. It is very likely that both of these men would have achieved top leadership without going through the leadership-training program. Morris told me that the training he received in Baltimore gave him the pathway to the top positions in New York City.

Morton L. Mandel was not only an enormously successful business leader, but served as Chairman of the Board of Cleveland JCF, President of the National Jewish Welfare Board, and President of CJF. Morris W. Offit moved from Baltimore to New York and was a Vice President of Salomon Brothers and Chairman of his own investment bank. New York is a very competitive environment for leadership in the Jewish community. Nonetheless, Morris became Chairman of the Board of UJA-Federation, New York City. Among many other leadership posts he held was the Presidency of the Jewish Museum.

The professional training programs that I had the opportunity to create were in Cleveland, Pittsburgh and Baltimore, but I did have the opportunity to create one additional training program in South Florida. The first graduate of the Baltimore Institute for Jewish Communal service to become a Big 16 executive was Stephen H. Hoffman. He had given several years to CJF as its chief executive and had returned to Cleveland as the President of JCF.

The last training program I had was in the UJA Florida Regional Office, in a program I set up while consulting for UJA. Mark Terrill was recruited into this new program. When he graduated, Baltimore hired him for the AJCWF staff. In a very short time he became the President of the AJCWF.

Stephen H. Hoffman and Mark Terrill, my first and last professional training program graduates, became the Top of the Top.

Of course, there were others, and I always congratulate them. When asked, however, to give anecdotal evidence of the models of success, these men, Morton L. Mandel and Morris W. Offit, volunteer leaders, and Stephen H. Hoffman and Mark Terrill, professional leaders, make the case.

The "Support Foundation" creation has been an ongoing bulwark of third leg financing. Baltimore's AJCWF alone has had fifty-two created, worth approximately two hundred fifty million dollars. Of these, two are directly related to me. Betsy Krieger had created The Fund for Change, and Jean Krieger Kahn, and her husband, Marc, created the Bancroft Fund. Both of these are served by Karen Kriesberg as their Executive Director.

As is noted in the INTRODUCTION the UJA and the CJF merged into a single organization and is currently named the Jewish Federations of North America. Other changes have taken place. The Northwest Baltimore Corporation went out of business. The Institute of Jewish Communal Services is now part of the Darrell D. Friedman Institute for Professional Development with a much broader mission than the original Institute. Changing opportunities make for new developments.

Most interesting to me is what the ZK Fund has achieved after my departure. It is among the recognized leaders in innovative Baltimore community developments. I frequently receive communications congratulating me on what the ZK Fund has done and the plaudits it has received.

Betsy, Jean and Karen, yes, three vital women leaders, have gone beyond anything Zan or I could have imagined. They have made the ZK Fund the face of the AJCWF, and the Jewish community, in dealing with Baltimore's problems.

We could not have imagined such an amazing outcome to the idea and hope that we had thirty-three years ago. I am pleased that I have had the privilege of seeing it and being able to write about it.

Betsy Krieger created her own support foundation, "The Fund for Change," Karen Kreisberg, Executive Director, primarily advancing social advocacy.

Betsy Krieger

THE BANCROFT FOUNDATION, a support foundation created by Jean and Marc Kahn, Karen Kreisberg, Executive Director, supporting primarily environment and education programs.

Jean and Marc Kahn

Morton L. Mandel

Morris W. Offit
Photo from Special Collections, Sheridan Libra-
ries, Johns Hopkins University

Stephen H. Hoffman

Mark Terrill

A

B

C

D

H

I

J